Mary's idea of "The Playground" presents a word picture that our foster and relative kinship care providers instantly see and connect with. Many have commented on how this concept has completely changed the way they look at communication and relationships. "The Playground" will impact all of your relationships, helping you to really see and honor the people in your life, including yourself!

—*Karen Jason*, DIRECTOR, FOSTER KINSHIP CARE PROGRAM, MENDOCINO COLLEGE, UKIAH, CA

Ms. McMillan has come up with a simple, yet very useful concept on how to make relationships work. Her idea of "The Playground" struck me right away as the basic starting point of mutual respect when people need to work out issues together. I now use it in my work, and it has changed my approach toward that very difficult arena.

—*Andy Weiss*, FOUNDER AND MANAGER OF KPFZ COMMUNITY RADIO IN LAKE COUNTY, CA

Get inside your Relationships

Tools and strategies
for building attachments

Mary T. McMillan, MFT

GoldDust Publishing
Kelseyville, California, USA

Book Design and Typesetting: Colored Horse Studios, Ukiah, California
Copy Editors: Christy Wagner and Fran Ransley
Cover Design: Cathy Gale

ISBN: 978-0-9825491-0-0
Library of Congress Control Number: 2010907446

GoldDust Publishing
P.O. Box 1236
Kelseyville, CA 95451
GetInsideYourRelationships.info

For Martha

Acknowledgements

First and foremost, I am indebted to D. W. Winnicott, M.D., Peter Fonagy, Ph.D. and Mary Main, Ph.D., practitioners and scholars whose works I have studied and used. Their ideas have laid the groundwork for my practice as a therapist and teacher, and their philosophies and perspectives have informed the ideas in this book. My goal has been to simplify and apply what I learned from them.

The works of Daniel A. Hughes, Ph.D. and Dr. Thomas Gordon have been an inspiration and major source of information presented in this book. And I am indebted to my students and clients who have given me their trust and curiosity, with real problems and tough questions.

And I am grateful for the open eyes and critical reading from friends and colleagues who have kept me honest, especially Jim Lehman, Jeanette Miller, Catherine Rosoff, Lourdes Thuesen and Andy Weiss.

ॐ

A note about how this book is written: to deal with the inherent gender bias of the English language, I have used a variety of ways to manage the third person pronoun. Sometimes I use a plural pronoun where normally it would be singular. Other times I alternate, from one paragraph or story to another, between a female and a male pronoun.

Table of Contents

PREFACE

ORIGINALLY I SET out to write a textbook for the class I teach at the local junior college and I expected this to be a professional journey. But soon it became clear that I was writing in my personal classroom voice, and that writing this book, like teaching and doing therapy, would challenge me to integrate my own life experience with my professional perspective.

Before I was born, my father was trained to be a Roman Catholic priest and my mother was raised as a Jew. They treated their marriage as an opportunity to wage a frightening and bewildering holy war, and while I was growing up it was normal for me to feel conflicted and confused with everyone I knew. It wasn't until many years after I left home that I began to suspect that some relationships might be different from those I had witnessed and experienced with my parents.

After pursuing four different careers and spending many years in school, I went into psychoanalysis. While being treated, I was also studying. I read the works of many psychoanalysts and became especially interested in object relations. During these years, I gradually changed my style of relating to others, transforming my family's foibles into what I now call the respectful relationship.

In 2003, while this transformation was still happening, I discovered attachment theory. I saw in this theory a clear, practical and profoundly effective explanation of how relationships affect and even define our potential for development as human beings. Elaborating upon D. W. Winnicott's concept of the playground and building on research from attachment theorists, I gradually saw the respectful relationship emerging as a concept with a definite shape. I included it in my curriculum at the college and added it to my therapeutic method in private practice. I also developed tools to help people put the idea into practice.

I soon became aware of how students and clients were responding: it was as if they'd held and even cherished this idea — maybe even before they could articulate it — but had forgotten or lost it as they had grown up. Immediately after I would draw a diagram of the respectful relationship and explain its rules, I would see looks of recognition — and belief.

My students are mostly parents and teachers, and the class focuses on improving relationships with children. Inevitably, during the first two meetings, they ask for quick solutions, reluctant to consider that their problems occur while they are relating to the children, and they might need to change those relationships. But by the last class, as they grasp and apply the rules of the respectful relationship and understand how to maintain it, many are amazed to discover that their most persistent relationship problems have disappeared — not only with children but with everyone. As I have seen my ideas and tools produce immediate and profound benefits, I have grown increasingly convinced that many people, if they had this book, would be willing to do the work required to improve or transform their relationships.

While I am teaching and doing therapy — as I do in my writing — I present my ideas in a factual, optimistic style. While they're learning about the different relationship styles, students and clients are often reminded of bitter or hard feelings — feelings that they may have wanted to forget. But I have found that when these feelings occur in a context that is matter-of-fact and hopeful, they often feel a new spark — they recognize a truth they can use — and they are encouraged to continue working.

People need a simple, clear and optimistic way of seeing—and solving—their problems. In writing this book, my goal was to provide a practical guide for people interested in building secure, durable relationships, and to offer hope to people experiencing trouble as well as the professionals who are helping them to cope. I would like to think that this book meets that goal.

INTRODUCTION

Getting inside relationships

MOST BOOKS ABOUT relationships offer advice about how to behave, such as "Listen empathically," or "Go with the flow." This advice isn't bad, but it's very general, and doesn't relate to the specific problems in our personal relationships. When I have a problem, I want to get inside my relationship and make a choice about how I—in my own unique way—should behave with this particular person.

Perhaps I'm involved in an important relationship and I don't want to break or damage it, but I do want my wishes to be respected. I may wish that we didn't argue so much. Maybe I have been involved with someone for a long time, only to discover that I never really knew him at all. A person could be very attractive to me, but for some reason I'm afraid to get involved. Maybe my feelings change from one extreme to the other. I might want to deepen an intimate connection, but I just don't know how.

Whether we're starting a new relationship or dealing with an existing one, we will want it to feel good and last a long time. If it's with a new person—a friend, colleague or lover—we may try to learn from our past mistakes. If we're discontented with an ongoing one, and it's too valuable to abandon, we will want to improve or repair it.

How do we start or change a relationship? Metaphorically, if the relationship were a room in my house, I would need to see the pieces of furniture—existing or in my past—from a different perspective. Inside our relationships, our internal furniture consists of our habits, thoughts and beliefs. They determine how we will feel and behave.

When I can see—and trust—this internal furniture, I can see my choices and know what I want. In any given relationship, if I decide to change my behavior by choice instead of trying to follow someone else's advice, I will be much more likely to get the result I want.

How can we see our internal furniture? To begin with, the thoughts and beliefs inside all human relationships are built upon one simple principle: to survive, humans need to feel attached to someone or something. Because attaching is such a crucial need, we have developed specific ways to connect to other people or things—either in reality, or in our imaginations. We cannot choose whether or not to attach, but we can choose how to.

In this book we will see that many people who have troubled relationships have unknowingly used their imaginations to manufacture their internal furniture. But all of us can learn to avoid this pitfall by building internal furniture that is real. To begin doing that, we need to know what respect is.

Respect

Most people want to feel respected and intend to treat others with respect. Relationships that feel good and last a long time are founded in this kind of mutual respect. But... what is respect?

In this book, we will examine respect—what it is and what it is not. We will get inside the four kinds of relationships in which humans feel attached, and we'll see clearly how respect works in the kind of relationship that lasts.

Like Leonardo da Vinci, who dissected the human body to learn about muscles and bones, we will dissect human relationships. We will identify their various parts and learn how they are the same, and how they are different from each other. We will discover the thoughts and beliefs that are determining our behavior, and broaden our choices about how we relate to others.

This book

This book is addressed to people who are curious about relationships or who want to change existing relationships or start new ones—and to helping professionals. My aim has been to describe, in down to earth language, the most useful strategies and tools people need to begin, maintain and repair relationships.

In the first part of this book, we will examine the four relationship styles and—step by step—learn to use the tools for building a relationship that is secure and lasts a long time. In the second part, we will explore strategies for keeping that secure relationship alive and running smoothly. In the third part, we will discover how to avoid damaging good relationships, and find tools for repairing relationships that have been damaged.

PART I

RELATIONSHIP STYLES

OUR FIRST RELATIONSHIP

IN THE KIND of relationship a mother has with her newborn baby, the mother and baby become merged emotionally. There is no mother without a baby, and there is no baby without a mother. If the parent doesn't respond to the baby, the baby will not thrive. But if the parent responds to the baby with love, they will merge—become emotionally one person.

SEPARATION

Ironically, while the baby's task is to attach to the parent during her first four or five years, the task of the parent will be to gradually separate from the child. I draw a picture of this process to help you understand a related idea in a later section.

First, Mother and Baby are, essentially, one person:

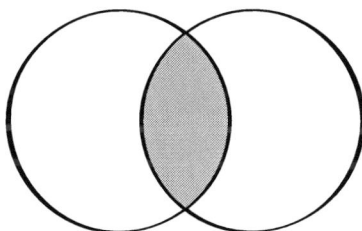

Gradually, they separate into individuals.

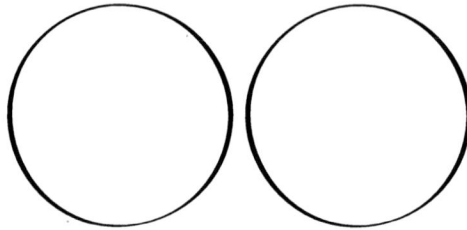

During the first five years, this separating process occurs in a certain sequence—a sequence that deepens the trust between each person.

THE SEPARATION PROCESS

1) The feeling of being a merged person develops first into an experience of sometimes being able to influence or control the other person.

2) Then the trust deepens, as each person enjoys being alone, preoccupied with his own world, in the presence of the other person.

3) Finally, the time comes when each person sometimes feels independent of the other.[1] One day the child might say, "I can tie my own shoes." He will want to—and the parent may expect him to—practice taking care of himself.

This doesn't mean the parent expects the child to take complete care of himself. It means that the parent respects the child enough to know how much he really can do, and encourages him to enjoy taking care of himself.

IN LOVE

Like a newborn and mother, two adults who fall in love feel that they are part of each other. While we are falling in love, we feel that we have become a whole new person—who exists only because we are part of the other person.

But over a period of time, the same sequence of separation that happens between newborn and mother happens between lovers. The period of infatuation protects the lovers while they develop and deepen their trust in each other.

And within two or three years, this infatuation fades. It changes into a more realistic understanding that this special relationship may provide something that was missing, and the other person may help us feel enriched or more complete. But we are not a new person. We still have the same old habits. To make sure this relationship will endure, we will need to do the work of building and maintaining a respectful relationship.

THE RESPECTFUL RELATIONSHIP STYLE:
A SECURE PLAYGROUND

THE RESPECTFUL RELATIONSHIP style is secure and can last a long time, because in this relationship style we can feel sure that we are accepted, we can grow as individuals, and we can protect ourselves from being harmed or harming the other person.

This relationship is a virtual place between two individuals who share the space as though it were a playground. We enter the relationship—the playground—to be with each other. I call the relationship a playground because what human beings do with each other in healthy relationships is play.

By play I mean interact and communicate—with both words and bodies. When I'm playing respectfully with another person, if he behaves in an unexpected way, I am surprised, and want to learn more about him. While playing, I want to explore—all the parts of my environment and the people in it. I feel free to think and express myself in creative ways—to discover more about who I am.

Playing is a ubiquitous human activity. Even when we are working, we are playing. In our families and in society, we play many very complicated—and sometimes serious—games with each other. Not all games have winners and losers—some exist as a way to get acquainted. Some are games where losing can mean death. But if we follow the rules of the respectful relationship, we are much less likely to get hurt.

The respectful relationship looks like this:

PLAYGROUND

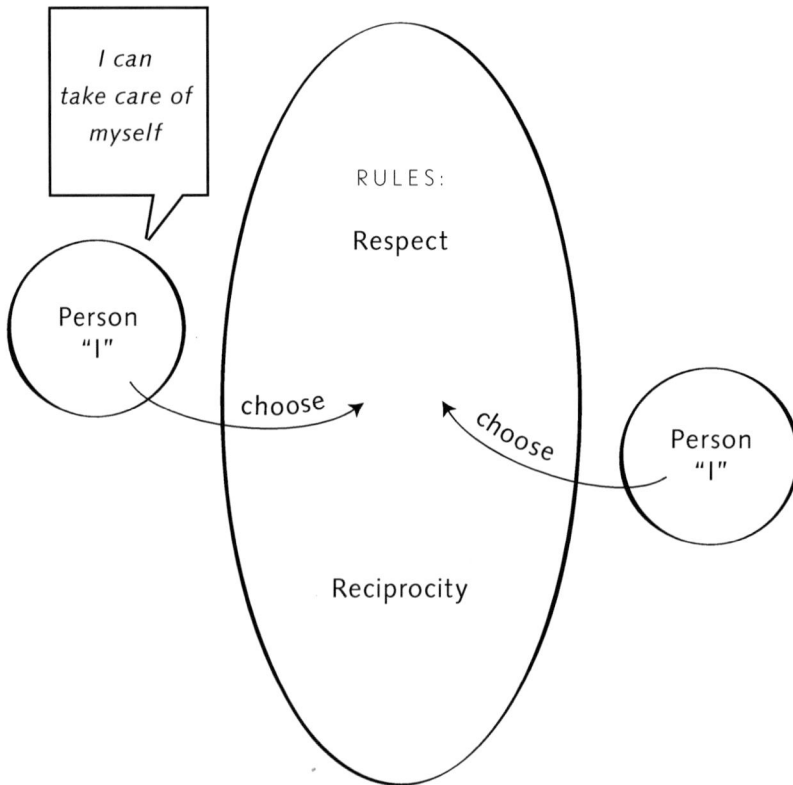

HOW THE RESPECTFUL RELATIONSHIP WORKS

THE RESPECTFUL RELATIONSHIP begins with two people who know they are separate from each other. Each person has an "I," a private part of the self. Each person's "I" defines and protects her own space. With her "I," she observes herself and the world around her; and she makes choices about how to behave, what to focus on, where to go and how much time to spend doing things.

AN IMAGE

The playground is not a prison or a heaven where we stay. It's a limited time and space that we share with another person, but the space does not need to be physical. In this modern age, we can play with each other in any number of virtual ways using our electronic gadgets, as well as just using our imaginations.

When we play with another person in a virtual way, we are calling upon an image of that person. While we talk on the phone our hands are often gesturing as though the other person were physically present, but in fact our playground is a space, and the person is an image, in our minds.

I don't need the telephone to consult my mother. Every time I ask myself, "What would she do?" I am entering a playground in my mind where I consult with my image of her. This image was planted there when I was an infant, and has evolved over the years.

Creating an image of each person in our lives is an important part of creating relationships with them. We can recall and play with our images—a process we call "remembering" or "thinking of" people—because they are planted in our memories. These images are as alive as we are. They appear in our dreams. They can grow and shrink and we can discard them, but they can never leave us and cannot be taken away. They belong to us. My image of my mother was probably my very first possession, and it will die only when I die.

WE CHOOSE TO ENTER

When we are engaged in a respectful relationship, we go into the relationship—or playground—only when we choose to. No one can force us into the playground. We usually enter it when we are invited or we invite the other person.

We play together as long as we choose to. When we stop playing, we aren't abandoning the person. We can leave the relationship, we can go back to being alone, we can enter into another relationship, or we can continue playing with that person by playing with an image of them. We can play with that image any time we want to.

Respect

Inside the playground, we need to always keep in mind two basic rules. The first rule is:

Respect each other.

What does respect mean? Lots of people think that to respect someone means to be nice. Or to obey. Many times we use respect to mean look up to, or admire. Respect can mean any of these things.

But if we look at the history of the word, we see that it comes from the Latin word *spect,* which means to see or to observe, plus *re*, which means again. So in this book—when we are dealing with people in general—respect will mean: to look at the other person—and then to look again.

To look again does not mean to like or to love the other person. At its most everyday meaning, it simply means that we acknowledge the presence of the other person. When we meet or are interacting, we make eye contact, nod, wave or say hello. When we're dealing with clerks or servers or people on the street, we don't ignore or bump into them. As if we're dancing, we take care not to step on their toes. We acknowledge their existence.

When we are interacting with someone who isn't just an acquaintance, someone we see repeatedly and meaningfully, look again can mean something much deeper. It still means to see the other person—but now we want to see them for who they really are.

How do we know who a person really is? To begin with, we take care to notice how the person behaves, as well as what they say. When they say "I'll take the garbage out," is the garbage still stinking in the kitchen the next day?

This looking again can hurt—especially when we notice that the other person is really very different from who we want them to be, or they don't behave as we expect them to. Looking again can mean we feel disappointed or disillusioned.

But it can also be a big relief, especially when we see that the other person is not who we were afraid they were. And when we are engaged with someone supportive and loving who behaves in unexpected ways, we can feel delightfully surprised. Looking again can mean that we take from them a whole new vision of being in the world, and our own vision grows to include theirs.

DANGER

Sometimes we can't avoid dealing with someone who is dangerous, but being respectful toward that person—seeing them as they really are—can save us a lot of grief.

The meaning of the word respect in a dangerous situation may be difficult to grasp. Remember that for you to acknowledge the presence of someone in the playground, you do not need to like him or accept his behavior. When I say that respect means to see the other person as they really are, I'm referring to an objective way of seeing—with your eyes stripped of all your feelings—as a bird might see him.

Respecting a dangerous person—someone who intends to harm you—means that you acknowledge her behavior. When we discover that a roommate or co-worker, for instance, is stealing from us, or lying, we can respect that. That is, we don't ignore this behavior or pretend it's not true.

Dealing with a dangerous person we can't evict or ignore can be a big problem. Sometimes we try to solve this problem by expecting him to be who we want him to be, or who we think he *should* be. But that doesn't solve the problem. Furthermore, it's not respectful.

Instead, like we do when crossing a busy street, we can look both ways more than once. If we see a semi-truck coming, we can get out of the way. When we can't avoid being in a relationship with a dangerous person, we can at least be respectful by being very cautious. We can *expect* her to be who she really is.

The person may have some good qualities—few people are all bad. Conversely, few people are all good. Being respectful includes recognizing a person's dangerous qualities as well as their good qualities. We can protect ourselves by avoiding interactions that draw out the dangerous qualities of people we like. And we can focus on interactions that draw out the good qualities of people who are dangerous, while continuing to expect that in certain times and places, these people will try to hurt us.

SUMMARY OF RESPECT

Most of us know how it feels to be respected. I know when the other person is making an effort to see all of me, and respond to my strengths as well as my weaknesses.

We all appreciate it when someone acknowledges our whole being, not just what we say, or how we appear on the surface. This means that in the playground, I am noticing, not only the words you speak, but also your body language and your actions. Even a crook can appreciate it when someone acknowledges his dangerous qualities as being a part of who he is. And when you are dealing with someone who has difficulty saying exactly what he means, he will want you to look at his actions as well as his words, because his actions can speak volumes about how much—or how little—he cares about you or about the project you share.

It's not easy to respect a person. To respect someone, we need to be paying attention. And respect takes time—time to look again. Agreeing to pay attention and take your time is how you will show respect in your relationships.

Reciprocity

The first rule in the playground is to respect each other. The second rule is:

Be reciprocal in your interactions.

Reciprocity refers to a back-and-forth way of interacting. In electricity, it describes the energy generated when particles rub together. In the playground, reciprocity is the energy generated when two people are genuinely interested in each other. Being reciprocal in your interactions means that you both give and receive. Talk and listen. Instead of speaking to dominate the conversation, each person speaks expecting the other to respond, expressing his own point of view.

Also, one person is not being a martyr, doing all the giving, while the other only receives. We all need to feel that we can influence and be recognized by the important people in our lives, and in the respectful relationship, reciprocity is what makes this influence and recognition mutual. It ensures that when someone really needs to speak, the other person will be listening—and conversely, when someone really needs a message or a response, the other person will find a way to express herself.

Another way to understand reciprocity is to say it is not a solitary activity. When we throw a ball back and forth or play tennis, the play is reciprocal. Reciprocity happens with a real person—not an image in the mind. It describes something I do, not something I wish for or dream about.

Because reciprocity generates energy, a relationship with more reciprocity (or reciprocity that is shared in more dimensions—space and time, verbal and nonverbal, platonic and sexual) can feel more intense or deeper. For example, if we have a shared history, spend time together in the same place, and feel physically attracted, the opportunities for reciprocity are multiplied many times. When more reciprocity is shared, the relationship can be more significant.

We learn that the true meaning of reciprocity comes not from counting or calculating how much one or the other gives and receives. Rather it comes from how one gives and receives.

When interactions are reciprocal, people feel they belong in the relationship. It is this feeling of belonging that builds a secure foundation and makes the relationship strong. When we share our honest perceptions, whether they are different or similar, our perceptions are woven into the relationship, and our world feels substantial.

Most babies learn to reciprocate by the time they are nine months old: when the parent smiles at them, they will smile back. But as we grow older, reciprocity grows more involved. Giving and receiving become more like negotiating, bargaining, bartering. It becomes more important to communicate clearly. As we mature, we understand ourselves better, and are able to say what we prefer. If we keep our interactions reciprocal when we express our preferences, we will avoid misunderstanding each other or making false assumptions—mistakes that can damage the relationship. The relationship is much more likely to last.

As a relationship deepens, the ways we reciprocate deepen as well. We learn that the true meaning of reciprocity comes not from counting or calculating *how much* one or the other gives and receives. Rather it comes from *how* one gives and receives.

No matter what you may think of another person, it is how you behave toward them that will determine the quality of your relationship. When you give attention respectfully, you are much more likely to get the respect you want. The quality of love you find in others will be determined by the quality of love that you give. In other words, in a reciprocal relationship, you get what you give.

RECIPROCITY IS SUBTLE

Sometimes we find ourselves trying to relate to a person who seems to be playing by the rules of the playground—but we just feel uncomfortable with them. Maybe when we leave the conversation we feel drained. Or we feel that we have to put on an act. There could be long pauses when no one has anything to say.

When you don't know why a relationship is faltering, consider that possibly there is a failure in reciprocity. When reciprocity is working well, we pay attention to each other's unique cues and the secrets we share; and these cues and secrets are shared in the subtle quality of our nonverbal communication and words that are unique to this relationship. A person's body language and the energy they generate is sometimes impossible to talk about and very hard to see.

Maybe the other person keeps talking, rarely expressing curiosity or concern about you and your life. You may be interrupted often, or your body language ignored. If she needs someone to dump her anger onto, you could be a handy target.

On the other hand, maybe you aren't communicating clearly what you want, or how you see things. With this person, you may need to be more assertive. If the relationship feels unbalanced, there probably isn't quite enough reciprocity.

THE MARTYR

Many people—especially women—believe that caring for someone is a one-way street. They believe they are supposed to take care of the child or the spouse, and it's selfish to want or expect the other person to give something back. Although she feels miserable, the martyr gains satisfaction from believing that her misery is helping the other person.

Often authorities like parents or pastors have fostered her martyr role or she grew up knowing that taking care of others was how she would survive. In either case, she has developed a habitual way of relating that is not serving her well. Changing that habit could feel dangerous and alien at first.

It takes courage to change our habits, and finding that courage will take energy. But continuing to feel miserable takes energy, too. In the end, we choose which goal we want, and put our energy behind that goal. That is how we will change.

If a person isolates herself in a one-way role, she is neglecting the rule of reciprocity. She prevents herself—and the people she loves—from growing up and fully participating in a respectful relationship.

SUMMARY OF RECIPROCITY

Reciprocity describes how people respond to each other. It generates energy in a relationship, and the energy is more intense when people respond to each other in several different dimensions—nonverbal as well as verbal. Reciprocity builds a solid foundation for a secure relationship. It reduces misunderstandings and false assumptions.

On a deeper level, reciprocity refers not to *how much* we give or receive, but rather to *how* we give and receive. How you behave toward the other person often determines how he treats you. Remember that when interactions are reciprocal, you get what you give.

Because it includes body language, unique cues and the relationship's secret language, the quality of reciprocity in a relationship can be hard to see. When a relationship feels unbalanced, consider making it more reciprocal.

Some people believe that it's selfish to want the other person to appreciate their work and support. These people often have grown up as martyrs, taking care of others in order to survive. It takes a great deal of courage to change the habit of being in a one-way role.

Our own rules

Besides the two basic rules of respect and reciprocity, we each bring many other rules into the playground. To make a relationship work, we both need to know the rules we believe in, and communicate them effectively. And when there is a conflict, we need to understand and appreciate the other person's rules.

What are our rules? Each of us has developed principles that guide us through life. We don't always know exactly what they are, but we can get a glimpse of them when we examine the beliefs behind our actions. These principles, based in our beliefs, are our rules. They may be the basis for routines that get us through the day: we have to shower before we eat breakfast. They may be related to privileges or rights: rules about curfew and chores or knocking on doors before entering. They are also the basis for our assumptions about how other people should behave: people should say hello when they first come home, or be honest, or do no harm. My most personal rules stem from my beliefs about how I'm going to achieve my goal: in order to get a good grade, I have to study. If I want to look respectable to others, I have to respect myself.

In any relationship, it's inevitable that some of my rules will differ or even conflict with yours. But difference itself isn't a problem. To be in a relationship with someone whose rules are very different can be stimulating and exciting. Although we often feel our rules are absolute, they can become remarkably flexible when we discuss them. While we are negotiating rules we can learn a great deal about ourselves and the other person.

AGREE TO DISAGREE

Sometimes, if the other person doesn't agree with your rule and you can't negotiate a change, you can agree to disagree about that rule. For instance, one parent might believe that children should be supported and micromanaged. The other parent might believe children should be given responsibilities and pay consequences when the responsibility isn't fulfilled. These two parents will interact with their children in different ways, but by agreeing to disagree—respecting each other's rules—they will instill respect in the children.

Some people fall in love with a spouse who believes in a totally different political or religious system, commanding some very different rules. This couple may find themselves engaged in some heated discussions, but if they agree to disagree, the discussions can take on the quality of play and exploration. As a result, they can learn a great deal from each other and, over time, possibly shift some of their more rigid beliefs.

I can take care of myself

There is one more rule to consider in a respectful relationship. Before you even go into the playground, you need to believe:

I can take care of myself.

This rule is so important and so multi-dimensional that we will be exploring its meaning throughout the rest of this book. But at its most basic, "I can take care of myself" means that we don't go into the playground to take care of another person. And we don't go into the playground to be taken care of. In the playground we play: share, talk, explore, interact.

As an adult, "I can take care of myself" means that I can be organized and groom and feed myself. And on a deeper level, it means, "I can protect myself." It means I will make sure that we both understand and agree to follow the two basic rules: respect and reciprocity. As we saw earlier, protecting myself can also mean that I acknowledge when the other person is dangerous, and I will avoid certain interactions with her.

If I need to, when I am first getting to know someone, I can describe the playground and its rules. If the other person doesn't follow these rules, I can assert myself, or stand up for myself. Some people think that standing up for myself means blaming or accusing the other person. But in a respectful relationship, it means that I can communicate my own needs and wishes in a respectful way. We will learn more about how to assert ourselves in Part III.

ENFORCING RULES

Even in the closest and most harmonious relationships, disagreements or conflicts happen. But "I can take care of myself" means that during a conflict we observe the rules of respect and reciprocity. If the other person ignores these rules, I can remind him. If he continues after being reminded, I can stop playing with him. I can let him know, "When you are ready to follow the rules, I will return." Sometimes this means that I spend some time being alone.

Being alone

As you can see, "I can take care of myself" implies that I'm not afraid to be alone. In fact, we can more effectively take care of ourselves if we actually enjoy spending time alone, cherishing the opportunity to be creative, to get to know ourselves or just relax and enjoy a hobby or a good book. When we are alone, we can become absorbed playing with the images of important people in our lives.

But many people feel guilty or afraid being alone. Some believe being alone is selfish. When they're alone, some may feel they have somehow failed, and are not lovable. Some people can't keep the images of important people in their minds, so when they're alone and don't have these images to play with, they feel abandoned.

People who grow up expecting to give themselves in relationships without receiving acknowledgement or appreciation—taking care of children or spouse, house or garden—feel selfish when they are alone and, instead of exploring their own preferences, will focus attention on what others might need. In fact, however, a person who enjoys giving himself as housekeeper or parent can develop a healthy appreciation for the peace that comes from being alone. While he's alone, he can appreciate the many ways the house is actually giving back—mirroring all his care, reflecting those clean counters and orderly shelves. A garden, by blooming and growing, can nurture anyone who cares for it—if the caretaker is willing to receive those gifts. Children and a spouse can be equally rewarding, if the person is only willing to acknowledge and receive their appreciation for his attention and hard work. In order for him to receive these gifts, however, the person needs to have some idea of what is going on in his mind. He needs to develop his "I."

MY "I"

My "I" is the home inside myself, where I go when I leave the playground—when I am alone. It is my private subjective self. It may be hard to imagine, but my "I" is not something I can ever fully share. My "I" is a part of me that develops when I'm an infant, and grows stronger and more effective as I become involved in relationships and adapt to different environments.

My "I" has two basic jobs: to observe and to choose. As an observer, my "I" looks at both the environment around me; and also at my own feelings, thoughts and beliefs, seeing them in the context of my experiences and my memories.

My "I" also makes choices. It chooses, at any given moment, which feeling or thought to focus on, and which to suppress—or put aside until later. These focusing and suppressing choices regulate my emotions, calming me when I start to get upset, or stimulating me, finding something interesting to explore, when I get bored.

In any given situation, my "I" controls my behavior by choosing how to behave. My "I" chooses which action will most effectively achieve my goal, or acquire what I want. It is my "I" who chooses whether and when to enter into a relationship and how to behave in that relationship.

Looking again at the rule "I can take care of myself," I could say that one of the most important meanings of this rule is that my "I" knows what I prefer, and sees the difference between realities and wishes, so that in the playground I can take care of myself by turning my preferences into real action.

Here is a picture of how the "I" looks in the mind:

THE MIND

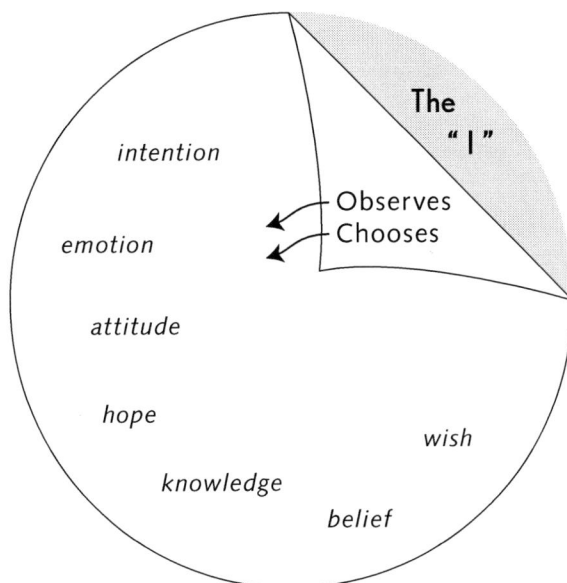

NURTURING THE "I"

For someone who dislikes being alone or taking care of himself, the respectful relationship might look like a lonely place. But in fact, this kind of relationship is much less lonely than the others.

When I engage in respectful relationships, I am nurturing my "I." As I play with someone in a respectful way and engage in reciprocal conversations, my "I" is constantly creating new observations and choices: it is growing. So when I return to the comfortable, secure home inside myself, I have added perspectives. Maybe I've learned something new about my preferences or interests, changed the way I see the world and other people.

When I stop playing in the relationship, I can be alone: I can go to my home—my "I"—whenever I want to. In my mind, I can play with the image of anybody: the person I just left or another person. Or I can choose to enter another playground—be in another relationship. And I can invite someone into a respectful relationship.

THE ROLE OF LISTENING

If you want to invite someone into a respectful relationship, all you have to do is listen. Listen respectfully and be interested, and most people will respond respectfully. If they don't respond right away, you may need to be patient, and keep trying. Someone who has been hurt in relationships may take a long time to trust you, but it is only if you are listening that you will have a chance to earn her trust. Listening is the best way to invite anyone into the playground. We will look more closely at listening in Part II.

RELATIONSHIP STYLES AS TEMPLATES

What determines the style of relationship we will have with other people? Relationship styles are learned at home when we're young, and we take them—like templates—into the world when we leave home.[2] Through these templates, we see the world. Unless we learn a new style, we expect all relationships to be like ours, and we can't even see that other people's relationships might be different.

If our relationships with both parents were respectful, then we will know how to engage in respectful relationships with our peers in school when we're young, and then, as we mature, with friends and with lovers and with colleagues and co-workers. We'll be respectful with clerks and servers and janitors. It will be our style.

Summary of how the respectful relationship works

The respectful relationship starts out with two individuals who choose to enter the playground: to be in a relationship. In this playground there are two basic rules. The first rule is: respect each other.

Respect means to look at the other person, and then to look again. In more significant relationships it means to see the other person—the way they really are. Sometimes we can't avoid being in a relationship with someone who cannot be trusted or wants to do harm, but we can protect ourselves by respecting that person: seeing her as dangerous, and not trying to change or ignore her bad behavior.

The second basic rule in the playground is: be reciprocal in your interactions.

Reciprocal interactions go back and forth—people respond to each other. As a relationship deepens, it can also mean that you get what you give. Being a martyr—caring for someone without expecting acknowledgment or appreciation—is a common way of breaking the rule of reciprocity.

In addition to the two basic rules, there are many other rules in the playground, because we each bring our own rules with us. Getting acquainted with each other's rules is part of what we do as we play together. Our individual rules can be negotiated or changed.

Before we even go into the playground, we need to believe: "I can take care of myself."

"I can take care of myself" means that I can organize and feed and groom myself; and I can enforce the rules of the playground. I can protect myself, or stand up for myself, if I need to. And if the other person is not following the rules, I can leave the playground.

Part of taking care of myself means that I appreciate time I spend alone. When I'm alone, I can continue playing with someone by playing with my image of that person. I can take that image with me everywhere, for the rest of my life.

Participating in respectful relationships nurtures the "I," which is that part of me who observes (myself and others) and makes choices. My "I" regulates my emotions and controls my behavior.

Our relationship style is acquired when we are young, and we take it with us when we leave home. It is the template through which we see the world.

Questions about the respectful relationship and how it works

The respectful relationship is like a playground because what we do with each other is play. What are some of the ways we play?

What are the two basic rules in the playground?

What does respect mean?

What does reciprocity mean?

What are two ways we take care of ourselves in the playground?

How can we continue playing with someone after we leave the playground?

Where can we go when we leave the playground?

What are the two main jobs of the "I"?

How do we invite someone into the playground?

THE INSECURE RELATIONSHIP STYLES

RESEARCHERS HAVE DISCOVERED that human beings relate to each other in four different styles. In the style we just examined, the respectful relationship, we can feel secure. That is, we can feel sure that we are accepted as we are, and we can grow as individuals. We can communicate our feelings and thoughts in words and gestures, and we can control our behavior. We can protect ourselves from being harmed or harming the other person.

But if we engage in one of the relationship styles we will examine next, we will feel insecure. In these relationships, we will never feel accepted for who we really are, and we cannot grow as individuals. We cannot play: we cannot explore or create freely. If we try to play, we will be harmed, or we will hurt the other person.

The most basic difference between the respectful and insecure relationships is that in the insecure relationships, there is no playground. There is no space or time for you to play; no way to say, "Wait a minute. You're breaking a rule." There's no place for growing and changing, and you cannot protect yourself from harmful behaviors.

An insecure relationship is not always easy to recognize. You can't identify it just by looking at certain behaviors. Indeed, as I describe these styles, even if you are engaged in respectful relationships, you might recognize some of your own behaviors. People in respectful relationships do sometimes behave in harmful ways because everyone develops bad habits. But these bad habits alone don't mean you are in an insecure relationship. We will look closely at bad habits in Part III.

In insecure relationships, words are used, not to express feelings in conscious or purposeful ways, but to obfuscate or hide feelings. People act out their hidden feelings in behaviors, and these behaviors pass for communication. In these relationships, acting out feelings (instead of using words to express them) is not an occasional lapse, but an entrenched habit. It is not the exception; it is the rule. For people trapped in these relationship styles, using words to hide their feelings, and then acting out their feelings in harmful behaviors, is how they live.

The intrusive or dismissive relationship style

In the intrusive or dismissive relationship style, both people feel that they are part of the other person. They believe they are sharing their whole private selves, even when they're not physically together. They each believe, "The other person is just like me and differences between us should not exist."

HOW THE INTRUSIVE OR DISMISSIVE RELATIONSHIP LOOKS

The intrusive or dismissive relationship might look familiar. It looks like the relationship between a mother and her infant, as we've seen before:

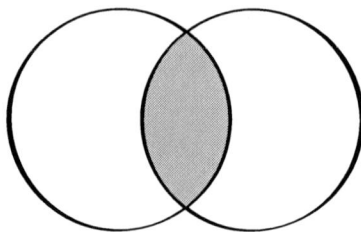

As you can see, there is no playground. There are no rules. The individuals are not separate.

As we've seen before, this relationship style can work, and is even necessary, in two situations: between a mother and her infant, and between two people who are falling in love. But in any other situation, the belief underlying this style—that "the other person is just like me"—is an illusion. It's an illusion we can find comforting—as long as we ignore all the problems it causes.

Sometimes the intrusive or dismissive relationship develops between a mother and her child—or between lovers who are no longer infatuated—when one or both people don't let the relationship change. They don't let themselves or the other person separate.

INTRUSIVE

In the intrusive relationship, privacy is being invaded. Neither person feels genuinely separate from the other, so boundaries, both physical and mental, are confused. In this relationship, I'm not sure where I stop and the other person begins. I often believe I own the other person—and everything that person owns. We constantly interrupt each other. I don't need to ask questions; I can just invade your privacy. For instance, if I want to know something about you, I will not ask questions; instead I will act out my questions by opening private drawers, reading diaries or mail, listening to messages, examining bills, etc. I might pull strangers or other relatives into our disputes. We have no secrets from each other or even strangers because there are no boundaries. In the intrusive relationship, any time you are behaving unexpectedly, I will demand that you behave as I want you to, but instead of making a direct demand, I will accuse you of behaving the wrong way.

You will recognize this style of relationship when you see two people who act like they should be able to read each other's minds. When one person wants something, he feels insulted if he has to ask for it—believing that the other person should already know what he wants. Instead of discussing or negotiating issues, people in intrusive relationships will manipulate or control each other—and each other's business or projects or relationships.

Instead of engaging in reciprocal conversations, one person will interrupt and dominate the conversation, and often the two will end up yelling. Or they may gaze into each other's eyes. Instead of stating what they want, they will argue, fight or glare.

Physically, both people often feel the other person's body belongs to them, which causes violence. When one person feels bad, she sometimes won't hesitate to hit, push, wound or even kill the other. Sometimes people involved in this kind of relationship will wound or try to kill themselves.

Dismissing can be subtle. If I am an assertive person and I'm working or talking with another person who isn't very assertive, it's likely that I will dismiss him.

DISMISSIVE

In addition to the intrusive version, this insecure relationship style also has a slightly different version, like a different flavor, called dismissive. Dismissing means getting rid of a person or an important problem without acknowledging them. In this version one person's needs are ignored most of the time. If I try to complain, the other person just interrupts or changes the subject. Sometimes, if I say I need something, like "I'm hungry," the other person might respond, "No you aren't," or "That's ridiculous." When someone objects to my behavior I might retort, "You don't understand," and walk away, or roll my eyes.

People in the dismissive relationship still believe that differences should not exist. "The other person should be able to read my mind. The other person is just like me." But while in the intrusive relationship, people will demand that differences disappear, in the dismissive relationship the people believe, "This difference is offensive so it doesn't really exist. I'll dismiss it."

Dismissing can be subtle. If I am an assertive person and I'm working or talking with another person who isn't very assertive, it's likely that I will dismiss him. An unassertive person often communicates nonverbally, with body language that is very easy to overlook. When I am focused on my own idea about where the conversation should go, I may ignore his fidgeting or looking around or other nonverbal cues that he's ready to change the subject. It's not my intent to dismiss him. But it happens often between someone who's assertive, and someone who is not.

In a respectful relationship, this dismissive behavior could be discussed and fixed: I could apologize, and he would feel validated. But if an unassertive person is stuck in a relationship that is dismissive, he cannot hope to ever be recognized.

THE EFFECTS OF THE INTRUSIVE OR DISMISSIVE RELATIONSHIP

When people have grown up in an intrusive or dismissive relationship, although they believe they are just like the other person, they feel uncomfortable in this relationship, and want to avoid the other person.

As they grow up, they expect other people to invade their privacy or dismiss them, so they tend to avoid relationships altogether. You can recognize children who are trapped in this kind of relationship when they become attached to their toys rather than to other children. They will ignore or avoid the teacher. During recess, they will play with trucks or dolls or computers, not other children.

Because they grew up often being interrupted, adolescents and adults who were trapped in intrusive relationships as children will often find they have trouble focusing. Images or thoughts may keep interrupting them—arriving out of the blue—and they have no control over these interruptions. These intrusive thoughts or memories can become very irritating.

Adults who grew up in this kind of relationship will isolate themselves. At work, becoming involved in structured projects with traditional rules and limits can substitute for the frightening prospect of having to navigate the territory of unique and unpredictable human relationships. Relationships with co-workers may be protected by company protocol or established routines, so they can stay superficial and safe from harm. At home these people may occasionally become involved in fleeting relationships that are intrusive or dismissive—until they get hurt. Their more long-term relationships will likely be virtual. They will probably spend a lot of time watching TV or movies or surfing the Internet.

Many people who fear their privacy will be invaded will become attached to things, instead of people. Food may become a substitute for companionship rather than a source of nutrition. A car might represent not a means of transportation, but a possession that connects them to the marketplace. They might depend on avatars in video games to make them feel involved in the world.

And many times, they become attached to money. While for people involved in respectful relationships, money can be a form of currency that flows through their playground and provides necessities and comforts, for people who fear invasion or dismissal, the marketplace may be the only playground that feels safe. Rather than communicating with a personal language of emotions and thoughts, they prefer to communicate by exchanging money. Money can serve as a mirror of their worth, so that they feel only as worthwhile as the amount of money they own.

The preoccupied or neglectful relationship style

In the preoccupied or neglectful relationship, one person is absent, preoccupied or neglectful. Often this person is too busy, working all the time or preoccupied with problems. Sometimes she is depressed or anxious, preoccupied with her misery or suffering. Sometimes she is addicted to substances like drugs or alcohol, or possibly addicted to gambling or some other activity.

The other person in this relationship, while being neglected, is utterly preoccupied with the person ignoring him. All of his attention and energy is consumed in wishing that the other person would acknowledge or recognize him, searching for any sign that she is aware of his existence. Since this is such a painful experience, he will spend a lot of time feeling frustrated and angry, or zoning out into daydreams.

HOW THE PREOCCUPIED OR NEGLECTFUL RELATIONSHIP LOOKS

absent or preoccupied person

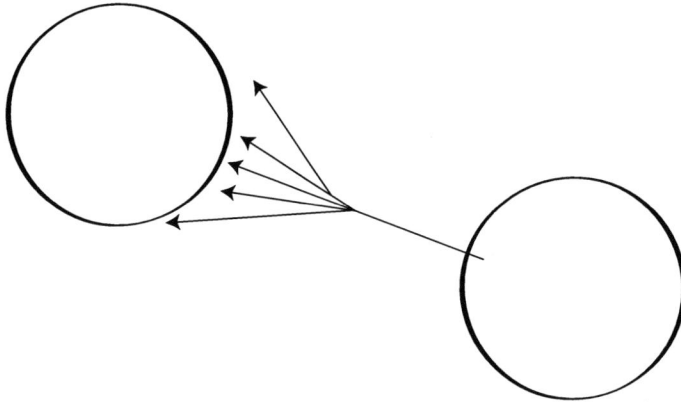

neglected person

In this style, both people are preoccupied. The absent or neglectful person is preoccupied with her own work, suffering, drugs, or worry. She feels consumed with just surviving and meeting her own needs, and the prospect of having to pay attention to someone else feels overwhelming. Ironically, however, she needs the neglected person the way a tree needs the soil. Although she doesn't want him around, she uses him. Without being aware of it, she might depend on him to provide her with the illusion that she is not alone. She could assume that he will defend her when she makes a mistake. Often she expects him to assert her preferences in the world.

The neglected person also needs the preoccupied or absent one. He is preoccupied with worrying about her, or wishes that he could get her attention. In his mind, he creates a function for her out of the empty space between them, and he does this in many ways. He will console or feed her. He could be a child who tries to function as the parent in the house, earning money and caring for siblings. He might be the spouse who makes excuses for her absences. He survives by turning himself inside out, transforming his need for attention into the work of being a crutch and paying attention to her.

While in the intrusive relationship there are no secrets, in this relationship there are only secrets. Both people keep secret—from themselves and from each other—the loneliness of the empty space between them. To protect this secret from others, they will isolate themselves, so that if police officer or neighbor comes to the door, the door will probably not be answered.

You can recognize a child as the neglected person in this kind of relationship when he sits in school and daydreams or worries all day. He cannot throw himself into a project or play with others. He cannot concentrate on schoolwork. Adults who were trapped in this style as children feel preoccupied and overwhelmed. While they may wish for some solitude, they cannot bear to be alone, feeling abandoned or worried when the other person is away. It is the man who can never trust that his wife will support him when he needs her. It is the person who always falls in love with someone who is married or not available.

EFFECTS OF THE PREOCCUPIED OR NEGLECTFUL RELATIONSHIP

In the intrusive or dismissive relationship, the people feel uncomfortable together and want to avoid each other, but in the preoccupied or neglectful relationship, the neglected person is utterly preoccupied with the desire to feel recognized by or close to other person.

When the neglected person is a child, the harm caused in this relationship is deep. The image he creates of the preoccupied parent can become an internal monster whom he hates, even while he wishes for her to pay attention to him. This internal monster can torment him for the rest of his life. Many of these children will become either bullies—in a vain attempt to vanquish that ghostly monster within—or chronic victims.

Children learn to form mental images of their parents during infancy, to help them feel safe. Most babies will focus on that image to soothe themselves, and help them remember that the parent will soon return. Later on, as adults, they form mental images of relatives, friends and lovers, and continue to rely on these images to help them feel connected and soothe themselves.

However, when a parent is absent for long periods—leaving the infant alone all day—the infant may never form that soothing mental image of a caretaker who will return. As an adult, then, she will tend to feel abandoned when she's alone, because she won't have this ability to form images that soothe her and help her feel connected. To feel safe, she will need to be physically present with her friends and lovers.

Children who are neglected tend to feel very ambivalent toward their parent. They will vacillate relentlessly between feeling extremely loving and extremely hateful. Later, as adults, they will vacillate between feeling hateful and loving toward their partners, their work, and their homes. They cannot settle into one feeling or the other. Every separation feels like the end of the world; they feel they're being abandoned forever, even if they know the separation will be brief. And then, when they are reunited with the other person, they are inconsolable—cannot stop clinging.

The disorganized relationship style

I will mention the fourth relationship style, the disorganized style, briefly, because it is rare. In this relationship, a child's behavior is not predictable, and the personality seems unorganized. It happens in families where children are seriously abused or neglected, or whose caretaker is mentally ill or traumatized. In these families, the child is confused because the parent is extremely conflicted in his feelings. The parent will follow an expression of violent anger (or other equally frightening behavior) toward the child with an expression of unrestrained guilty affection and reassurance. So the child is frightened by the same caretaker she depends on for reassurance and safety.

Children in other kinds of relationship styles, when they are frightened by their parents, have a solution to their fear: they can escape or hide. But in the disorganized style, because the child depends for reassurance and safety on the same parent who hurts her, she experiences an intense form of confusion—what Mary Main calls *fear without solution.*[3]

We can recognize children growing up in a disorganized relationship when their behavior with caretakers is relentlessly coercive and controlling, making teachers and other caretakers feel utterly helpless.[4] While with some adults they can be charmingly cooperative, they do not develop an abiding attachment to anyone or anything, but instead become attached to things or people that offer the most attractive opportunity at the moment. They will often leave the classroom without permission or run away from home.

Comparing the insecure relationships and the respectful relationship

Why would someone stay in an insecure relationship, even if they know about the respectful relationship?

In the insecure relationships, the attachment is insecure—people don't feel respected, and the relationship is built on illusions. Someone involved in this kind of relationship is only vaguely aware of what is going on in her mind. Her "I" has to peer through a thick fog of confusion and fear because her relationships are so troubled. Her "I" never gets to exercise and grow strong by playing with others, so it is small and undernourished. She can name very few of her emotions, thoughts or beliefs, and her behavior is determined mostly by habits instead of by making choices.

In these relationships, people always feel connected—not alone—even though that connection is only an illusion. In the intrusive/dismissive relationship, there are no boundaries; each person feels a part of the other, while simultaneously wanting to avoid the other. In the preoccupied/neglectful relationship, each person is preoccupied. One person is overwhelmed by the challenge of surviving; the other is worried about the overwhelmed person. But in both relationship styles, the people feel connected. This feeling of connection is an illusion the mind creates to keep the people from feeling alone.

To someone who is trapped in this illusion, the respectful relationship, where he would have to be a separate individual, choosing all by himself whether to participate in the playground, may appear unbearably lonely. Being involved in his insecure relationship feels like destiny, provided for him by a bigger reality. He doesn't choose if or how to participate in it. And he would much rather feel trapped in this illusion than face the fear of being a unique, separate individual. The prospect of having to make and express his own choices may feel akin to jumping out of an airplane without a parachute.

People in insecure relationships are bewildered about why relationships cause so much pain; and they fear being abandoned because their connections are never reinforced by reality and they never change. The illusion of being connected has to be vigilantly defended to keep it from disappearing.

WORRY IN INSECURE RELATIONSHIPS

Because people in insecure relationships are unsure of how real their connections are, they tend to worry a lot. Although they may think they are worrying about the other person's fidelity or fitness or any number of other things, at the basis of their worry is a fear that the other person will die or abandon them, and they will be stranded in outer space.

For these people, worry can become a companion—a companion in many ways more present and more pressing than the person with whom they feel connected. Worry is a frustrating and depressing companion, but it is at least a companion, and helps them feel less alone. In an odd way, worrying about the other person gives us the impression that we are in control. If my father is absent or preoccupied, I may worry that he will die. While I'm worrying, I believe that I am in control of his death. Worrying about him is how I love him and try to keep him attached to me.

The habit of worrying can become entrenched very early in a child's life. If I keep that habit later in life, I will continue to worry even when I'm with people who are paying attention to me. Worrying becomes how I love. It is a habit very hard to break.

ALWAYS AND NEVER ALONE

People in insecure relationships have not yet learned that as separate individuals, we are both always alone, and never alone. I am always alone in the two most significant relationships in my life—with Death and with God. In these relationships, I explore alone the mystery of the unknown, and all the dignity and joy I experience in this journey belongs only to me.

On the other hand, when I am respectful, I am never alone. I open my eyes to see and respect myself, including all the images and memories I hold in my mind, and engage my mind when I acknowledge others and respect the world around me. I am in a community of other people and the creatures, plants and environment that sustain us.

When we respectfully open our eyes, we can find ways to give to others, and we can receive their appreciation. We can explore the enigmatic questions that all people ask, share the mysterious beauty of people and places and creatures we love, and notice the fascinating ways our memories and intuition connect us to dimensions beyond our comprehension.

We can never be alone as long as we are engaged in the bigger reality, where the world turns, and seasons change. Stars light the sky without our having to ignite them. Creatures and plants respond to forces we can't control. We can contemplate the puzzles of God and Death and Justice and Love any time. We can open our hearts to be touched by passions in family and work dynamics, in art and religion, in politics and community.

Our images of the people, bodies, mysteries and cultural symbols in our universe belong to us. They are in the cupboards and drawers of our minds, whether we appreciate them or not. And we choose how to relate to them. If we are respectful of these images, honor their histories and pay attention to them, we will benefit from our relationships with them. They can feed our hearts and souls, and keep us warm in the winters of hard times.

Summary of insecure relationships

Unlike respectful relationships, insecure relationships don't have a playground with rules. In insecure relationships, words are used to hide discomfort; the "I" is undeveloped, so neither person can make choices about how to behave. Feelings get acted out in habitual behaviors.

INTRUSIVE OR DISMISSIVE

In intrusive or dismissive relationships, people believe, "The other person is just like me." If one person appears to be different from the other, that difference is not tolerated.

In intrusive relationships, there is no privacy, and there are no boundaries or secrets. People are constantly interrupted. If one person is different, the other will demand that she change. Instead of discussing differences, the people will manipulate, blame or try to control each other.

In dismissive relationships, differences between individuals are ignored or devalued. If one person expresses a problem, the other might say, "That's ridiculous."

People who have grown up feeling trapped in an intrusive or dismissive relationship will tend to avoid relationships. They will tend to become more attached to things, instead of people.

PREOCCUPIED OR NEGLECTFUL

In the preoccupied/neglectful relationship, one person is too busy, depressed, anxious or preoccupied with survival to pay attention. The other person is neglected, becomes preoccupied with worries, and wishes that she weren't being ignored.

Whereas in the intrusive/dismissive relationship there are no secrets, in this relationship there are only secrets. The absent or preoccupied person isn't aware how much she depends on the neglected person, who constantly worries or daydreams about the absent one.

People who have grown up trapped in this kind of relationship tend to vacillate between intense feelings of both love and hate toward others. They can't tolerate separation, and then can't stop clinging when reunited.

DISORGANIZED

The disorganized relationship is rare. It happens in families where children are seriously abused or neglected, or whose caretaker is mentally ill or traumatized. The parent will follow an expression of frightening behavior toward the child with an expression of unrestrained reassurance, leaving the child in an intense form of confusion called *fear without solution.*[5] Children growing up in a disorganized relationship are relentlessly coercive and controlling, making teachers and other caretakers feel utterly helpless.[6]

INSECURE VS. SECURE

Insecure relationships are called insecure because the people trapped in them fear being abandoned. In these relationships, we cannot tolerate feeling alone, so we create an illusion of feeling connected to others. But this connection, with no basis in reality, feels insecure.

On the other hand, respectful relationships can be called secure because people feel respected and the connections between them are always being reinforced in reciprocal interactions. These relationships can change and grow over time. We can build respectful relationships with many different people, and may even cherish time alone, when we can play with the images of others. We can appreciate the mystery of the unknown, and develop our own relationships with God and with Death that are satisfying and nurturing.

Questions about insecure relationships

What is the basic difference between secure relationships and insecure relationships?

How are intrusive and dismissive relationships the same? How are they different?

How do people communicate in insecure relationships?

If you were the neglected person in a preoccupied/neglectful relationship, how would you spend your time?

Why are insecure relationships called insecure? Why is the respectful relationship called secure?

PART II

MAINTAINING
THE RESPECTFUL
RELATIONSHIP

MAINTAINING THE RESPECTFUL RELATIONSHIP

The paradoxical nature of connection

AS WE'VE SEEN, a respectful relationship is like a playground. It's not a real playground that exists in space, but a way of connecting with people, sometimes in physical space, sometimes in virtual space, sometimes only with images in the mind. What makes the playground respectful is how people connect.

So when we're discussing maintenance of this playground, we're focusing not so much on who or what we play with, but how we play. How do we keep our relationship alive? How do we ensure the playground stays unique and fun to be in? How do we stay respectful and ensure the relationship doesn't evaporate as soon as a problem or difference arises between us?

The answer to these questions lies in the paradoxical nature of our connection. The connection I feel with you is as alive as we are, and yet it is elusive—it doesn't exist anywhere except in my own mind. And although the fact that I'm committed to this relationship doesn't change, this feeling of connection is always evolving—as I get to know you better and we both mature, the ways I see and think about you change over time.

So one way to think about this connection is to imagine it as a car, traveling across the landscape of the playground. As it represents our mutual, unchanging commitment to each other, the car does not change its shape, and we occupy it together.

But as it represents the nature of my connection with you, while I get to know you over time, the car changes its location, traveling across the living landscape of the playground. As we become better acquainted, we may notice that we're in different territory. Or we may revel in the comfortable familiarity of our surroundings.

We could further imagine that we are building the car's road while we travel. The road represents our form of communication—a road that is respectful. As occupants of the car, we are responsible for maintaining the particular road we are building together, and ensuring it doesn't disintegrate or become harmful.

So when we're talking about how to maintain and keep alive a respectful relationship, we're talking about how to maintain a road we are building together, while we cross the living landscape of the playground in our car.

During periods when our relationship is harmonious, we are comfortable with each other, and communication is direct and easy. We could say that during these harmonious periods, we are building freeways where we speed through time, hardly ever encountering an obstacle or a bump in the road.

But even in the most harmonious relationships, a time comes when the road becomes more difficult—bumpy or full of holes—and we have to slow down. Or we find ourselves in strange territory and feel lost. During these times, we may be experiencing conflicts or misunderstandings; or someone might be going through a change that stirs up frightening new emotions.

Tools for the road

The basic tool used to build roads in the landscape of the playground is as simple to use as a screwdriver, but there are many different kinds and sizes. This tool is called listening.

ATTUNED LISTENING

Most of the time we're hardly even aware that we're listening. When we're traveling along a freeway, in comfort and ease, both of us are attuned. Attuned means that we're on the same wavelength, like we're singing the same tune. We're listening to each other, reciprocating in our conversations. We may be sharing our secrets. We are acknowledging and respecting each other, and empathizing with each other. And we're sensitive to each other's body language.

This kind of listening is not exactly carefree, but it is fun. It's a little more involved and takes more effort than the conversation you might have with a clerk when you're buying a quart of milk. In a conversation where you are attuned, you are listening to each other, but also each person is listening to herself, the way someone singing a duet will listen to her own voice as well as that of the other.

All listening is akin to translating. We usually interpret the other person's words as something we expect to hear—we translate it into our own vocabulary.

All listening is akin to translating. We usually interpret the other person's words as something we expect to hear—we translate it into our own vocabulary. When the words surprise or hurt us, we will hesitate—the translation will take a little longer. In attuned listening, the translation is quick and works smoothly—I will understand what you mean and then translate my reaction into words or gestures that you in turn will understand. Most of us learn to do this kind of translating when we are young, and have to get an idea or request across to our parents. With our children, we might sometimes translate frustration into statements that are respectful.

On the freeway, as we converse, I am paying attention to how my body reacts to what you just said, and I am translating my reaction into something I want to say—to you.

This particular you-ness is another quality that makes attunement different from ordinary listening. When we're attuned, I am responding to you, not only as who are right now, but also as everything I know about you, and everything I would like to know about you. In this kind of listening, I'm weaving the present moment in with our history and our future together.

This kind of listening may sound complicated, but it is simple and it feels good. It doesn't require us to engage the whole body and mind. Once we get attuned, this kind of listening becomes a habit, something we do without working at it. It's like a simple flat head screwdriver.

ACTIVE LISTENING

When the road gets bumpy or we feel lost, however, the kind of listening we need to use is not so simple. When we suddenly realize we're not singing the same song, or one of us is off key, the first thing we need to do is slow down. We can speak more slowly. And we can think for a long time before we speak.

And we can also listen more slowly. Listening becomes more like a Phillips screwdriver: it has more facets, more ways to engage. When we listen like this, we engage the spirit, the mind and the body. This is called active listening.

Many authors have published books, tapes and other resources about how to practice active listening, and a list of some of these is included in the Appendix. In this book I want to describe active listening briefly, and focus on how to use it to maintain a respectful relationship.

But before we begin to examine active listening, let's look at the reason we need to use it.

The attachment sequence

One of the ironies of the respectful relationship is that separation is what keeps us together. Poets express this when they say that absence makes the heart grow fonder. We grow more attached to each other as we navigate the territory of separating and reuniting.

In psychological terms this means that attachment happens in a three-part sequence—a sequence that repeats itself over and over again. The sequence begins with attunement, the feeling of harmony that's like being in the car together on the freeway.

In the next sequence the inevitable happens: the attunement is disrupted. This disruption often happens when we're interrupted by reality. Maybe I have to leave you for longer than usual. Sometimes you might misunderstand what I'm saying, or misinterpret how I behaved. It could happen when one of us makes a mistake. When the attunement is disrupted, we are no longer singing the same tune.

The disruption period is a very important part of the attachment sequence. It's a time of feeling separated. It's a time when we can look more objectively, not only at ourselves, but also at our relationship.

During the disruption, I worry or wish about the relationship. In other words, I am outside of the relationship enough to observe it and possibly evaluate it, rather than simply being in it. In metaphorical terms, I might look at this old car and wonder if maybe I want to paint it, or buy a new one.

There are different kinds of disruptions. Along a continuum, some disruptions are minor, and some are more major. An example of a minor disruption might be if you have insulted my friend, and I believe we can quickly work out a plan to be sure this doesn't happen again. But if you have hauled off and hit me, I would consider this a major disruption. A major disruption may never be resolved, and can destroy the relationship.

Minor disruptions are inevitable and often provide an opportunity to strengthen the relationship. But if these minor disruptions are not discussed and resolved, they can build up over time into a major disruption. Some people tend to stay silent and stuff their resentments or hurt feelings—minor disruptions—into a mental backpack, one after another, until the load gets too heavy and the contents turn into one major disruption. A built up pile of unresolved disruptions like this can be quite destructive.

A minor disruption gives me an opportunity to look at this car we've been driving together: what is valuable about it, and what bothers me? It's during this period of disruption that, in one form or another, I have to answer the question, "Am I committed to this relationship?"

If the answer for both of us is yes, we will enter the last part of the attachment sequence: we will re-attune. That is, we will find a way to get back into the relationship. We will both find a way to sing the same tune again.

Here's a picture of the attachment sequence:

1. **Attune**: share, acknowledge, respect, empathize
   2. **Disruption**: a misunderstanding or interruption
      3. **Re-attune**: working to regain attunement

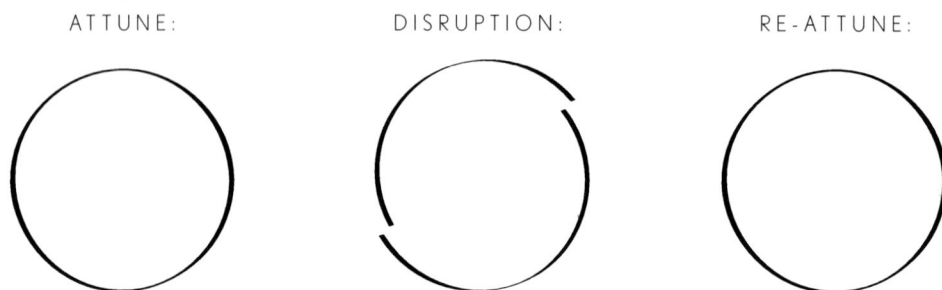

ATTUNE: DISRUPTION: RE-ATTUNE:

How do we re-attune? In metaphorical terms, I may need to listen carefully to your tune, and shift or alter mine just a little bit, so that we're both singing together again. Maybe I'll begin by apologizing or complaining. Maybe I'll ask you to shift your tune a little bit. Or maybe we're both tired of that old tune, and as we talk things over, we discover a whole new tune to sing together.

But how do we do that in reality? The answer will be different for each relationship, and for each disruption, but it will often involve active listening. Sometimes we may need to make a date and spend some unstressed time together. I could invite you to express your frustration, while I carefully listen. Maybe the problem will disappear quickly as we both realize we've been expecting too much. Or it might take a long time to examine exactly what the problem is, and make a plan to solve it.

GLUE OF ATTACHMENT

Ironically, the goal of attachment is to stay on the freeway of harmony and attunement, but the freeway is not what keeps us together. What keeps people together—the glue in relationships—is the process of working through the last two phases of the attachment sequence—disruption and re-attunement.

During the disruption phase, each of us will examine and then re-commit ourselves to the relationship. This disruption could be very mild or it could be intense. Sometimes it will take a few seconds; sometimes it will take days or even months or years.

Then, during the re-attunement phase, we will interact in a way that develops the trust and deepens the love that keeps us together. Again, this phase will take varying lengths of time.

The three-part attachment sequence happens again and again, at different levels of intensity, often many times a day. It is the constant repetition of this sequence that builds a strong attachment and keeps the relationship comfortable and fertile.

Using active listening to re-attune

In the playground, active listening is the tool most often used to reunite after a disruption. It's an excellent way to address and resolve whatever caused the disruption, to solve problems and to keep things running smoothly. This kind of listening is, in some ways, a hallmark of the playground.

In his book, *P.E.T., Parent Effectiveness Training*, Dr. Thomas Gordon writes thoroughly and usefully about active listening—what it is, and how to use it with children. In my explanation of active listening below, I am providing brief summaries of many of the concepts and techniques that are spelled out in detail in his book.

EXPLORING

Usually you will use active listening when the other person has a problem. He may come to you with a complaint or express a wish or he may need to talk about something bothering him.

If you didn't know about active listening before, when you were confronted with a complaint like this you might have used tools that didn't work very well—methods of communicating that would have avoided reciprocal conversation. These methods would have protected you from having to revise how you saw the problem. Dr. Gordon refers to these methods as "sending a solution message." They are messages saying, "I already have the solution, so we don't have to discuss what the real problem may be, or take time for you to explore possible solutions."

Unfortunately, taking this shortcut and solving the problem yourself cuts off the opportunity to discover the best solution. It also breaks a rule in the playground because it doesn't respect the possibility that the other person might have a different way of seeing things. In addition, a shortcut is not a reciprocal interaction.

Here's a list of shortcuts that we often use when confronted with a problem:

SHORTCUTS

1) lecturing   5) blaming
2) giving advice   6) praising or reassuring
3) giving directions   7) name-calling
4) threatening   8) sympathizing

Unfortunately, these methods don't foster reciprocity. They don't improve the relationship, and don't develop the other person's capacity for solving problems. Active listening, on the other hand, does foster reciprocity. Following is the basic method for exploring a problem when using active listening.

You can see in this sequence that when the other person has a problem, it is his job to fix it. But for many people, the hardest part of active listening will be giving up the belief that as the listener, it is your job to fix the problem.

It can be a huge relief for you to trust that the person who has the problem also, most likely, will know the best solution. What he needs from you, as a listener, is your support while he explores: for you to see the problem from his point of view, and then help him figure out what he thinks is the best way to solve it.

ACTIVE LISTENING

1) After the person complains or defines the problem, the two of you learn more about what the problem really is. When did it start? What are the feelings and thoughts behind it?

2) Once you both agree on what the problem is, you can explore what the possible solutions might be. The rule here is that the person with the problem knows more about it than you do. He is more likely to see—and follow through on—a good solution if you trust him to find it himself. If he needs some ideas, he can ask for them, but remember your role as listener is to support his exploration.

3) Once a few possible solutions have been discussed, the person with the problem is given the opportunity to select the best solution.

ATTITUDE OF ACCEPTANCE

Active listening requires, first and foremost, an attitude of acceptance. Adopting the accepting attitude is not something that happens automatically. To begin this kind of listening, we need to take some time to adjust ourselves. It's like putting on a thinking cap or a uniform: we get out of our automatic, subjective way of thinking.

Our automatic way of thinking is more like a reaction. In our culture, when we hear or see something different or challenging, often our first reaction is to fear it. When we're afraid, we will judge the different person or point of view. Judging her means we label her as good or bad. Judging immediately gives us distance and protects us from having to revise our perception.

But judging closes the mind. While we take a judging attitude, we are not listening. In order to open our minds and listen, we need to find courage—to not surrender to this fear of difference.

To give me courage, I adopt an accepting attitude—give the other person credit. I take time to adapt to her difference: a moment. Often, that moment gives me time to consider that possibly I'm afraid because I have to give up my belief that I can control her—and remember that the only person I can control is myself.

Active listening takes practice. It is a discipline, and learning when and how to use the methods can take some time. Active listening is slow. We take time to be objective and thoughtful. We take a moment to respond instead of react. We will alter our perception or adapt to reality if necessary. We can call this moment time to think.

THINKING

While attuned listening includes listening to myself, active listening adds an important element: thinking. When I have an accepting attitude, I insert a moment of thought between what you're saying, and what goes into my ears. I also insert thought between my reaction to what you're saying and what comes out of my mouth.

The first thought I insert is a reminder that I accept you the way you are. I care about your feelings and thoughts. I will to do my best to understand why you are saying this—and to respond in a way that honors our relationship and keeps our conversation going. I remember that the goal of my response is not to persuade you, but to learn: who are you, really?

VERBAL BREATHING

Another hard part of active listening is learning to be a good supporter during this exploration process. To be a good supporter, you take time to think before you respond. The pace of conversation can be quite slow. In this way, active listening is like breathing deeply. What you hear from and see in the other person is like air being breathed in: his words, tone of voice, posture and gestures and other body language. All that you hear and see is his message. You mix his message with your own understanding of its context and history and the meaning of all his body language. That is, you translate his message into your own language. Then you take time to think about all this: as much time as you need. When you are ready, you breathe out—you express your translation—saying or explaining what you have heard. Or you can ask for more information.

A person practicing active listening is very present and focused on what the other person is saying right now. And she is curious: she wants to know what the person means.

Another way of saying all this is that when you are listening, your "I" is alert. Its job is to manage your own reactions—your thoughts and feelings—while receiving and translating the other person's message. Your "I" will notice your reactions, but you won't express them—yet. You will use your reactions to help you understand and translate the message. But wait until later to express them.

A person practicing active listening is very present and focused on what the other person is saying right now. And she is curious: she wants to know what the person means. Sometimes in her response, she will translate what the other person can't put into words.

When I'm teaching active listening, most students find it impossible at first to focus on what I am saying without reacting. They immediately judge what I'm saying and want to tell me what they're thinking. I remind them to focus on accepting me and translating my message—or asking for more information—and I repeat what I was saying. This time they're able to insert that moment of thought—to respond, instead of react. Instead of judging me they can respond with something like, "You're feeling sad" or "Tell me more."

To learn active listening, many students practice with a spouse or someone else who can help them learn the discipline it takes to remember to insert that moment of thought, and practice the listening methods. Once they have mastered a few of the basic techniques, they often tell me that active listening has changed their lives. When they use it to maintain the roads of communication in their significant relationships—especially in relationships that have been painfully troubled—they successfully solve problems that have been plaguing them for years.

How does active listening affect the person doing the listening? For me, listening is fulfilling. When I am using this tool with you, I am taking in your most honest, passionate and important qualities, and then I am giving them back to you. Like verbal breathing, this process gives me an opportunity to take in a new or different way of seeing things. My listening allows us to connect in a way that is real and enduring. And this kind of connecting feels like love.

Active listening requires an attitude of acceptance. On the following page is a list of the basic qualities and facets of the accepting attitude:

THE ACCEPTING ATTITUDE

1) **Trust**: To begin with, I need to trust that you are a good person. Your behavior may be bad, but your intention is good. This is very important. Only with this basic trust can other trust develop. Also, I need to trust that you are capable of solving your own problems. This means I am not responsible for fixing your problems, but I do trust that if we both work together, I can see the problem from your point of view. And I can support your way of seeing and solving your own problems.

2) **Empathy**: I am putting myself in your shoes—not forever, but just long enough to understand your feelings or how you see the world. As I listen, I am drawing on my own experience, imagining how I might have felt and thought, had I been in your situation.

3) **Curiosity**: The beginning of curiosity is to believe that we are different from each other. I want to know how you are different, to understand who you are, really. What do you believe? What makes you behave as you do? What do you mean, exactly, when you say that?

4) **Respect**: In active listening, I work hard to acknowledge and accept everything about you, and to see you as you really are.

RULES OF THE ROAD

When we are traveling on the bumpy road, going slow in our relationship car, we are traveling in the landscape of the playground. The playground still has its two basic rules, but now the road is bumpy or someone feels lost. Either you come to me, or I confront you, with a problem. When trouble appears, it's a good idea to set aside some time to talk.

Here are some rules to consider when you do sit down to talk:

ACTIVE LISTENING METHOD

1) Give yourselves enough time
2) Prevent interruptions or distractions
3) Agree to respect each other
4) Stick to the present: do not delve into the past
5) Stick to the facts
6) Emotions are facts too. Express your own emotions in a respectful way

---

During an active listening discussion, the focus is different from ordinary conversation in the playground, where we would expect the conversation to be reciprocal. Although a very satisfying conversation can include both people practicing active listening usually, when we are using this tool to re-attune after a disruption, one person is doing most of the listening, and the other person is complaining, explaining or exploring.

The first goal during this discussion is to get the conversation started. It might be helpful to imagine that listening is like a door into the other person's reality. Sometimes, the first thing you have to do is get that door open.

DOOR OPENERS

The other person's reality may be as dark and unknown for him as it is for you. Often talking about my reality is like holding out a lamp and traveling into an attic full of unexamined problems and questions that I've been storing—sometimes all my life. The lamp I hold is the opportunity to talk about something that's bothering me.

It is usually when I talk about something bothering me that I can find these hidden-away problems. And here's a key: when the other person is listening—with an accepting attitude—I am able to listen to myself. This kind of conversation makes it possible for me to see these problems hanging around, and consider that they may even be causing whatever problem is bothering me. Then, if I'm ready, I can do something about them. This is why it's so important to talk with someone who really wants to accept me just the way I am.

Usually we use active listening when there is trouble. If someone comes to me with a problem, or I see a problem in our relationship, my first goal is to find out how she sees the problem. But the other person may have trouble talking about it, so I use a set of tools to open the door.

Body language

My first tool helps me hear what she cannot say: I pay attention to her body language. Almost all of our primary communication happens with our bodies. We learn to speak and to read body language long before we learn words. Paying attention to the other person's body language—throughout the conversation—is our primary way of listening.

The second set of tools helps me communicate the message, "I'm listening. I want to know more. I hear you."

Saying nothing

One of the simplest ways to communicate acceptance is to be patient: maintain eye contact and respect, while saying nothing. This gives him time to explore his own mind, without having to hurry.

Deep breathing

When a conversation is uncomfortable or frightening, and you are waiting for her to speak, it can help to just breathe deeply. Allow your breathing to calm you, and create an inviting space between you.

Phrases or sounds that communicate acceptance

"Hmmmm" is a sound that can, like saying nothing, communicate, "I'm listening."

"I see."

"Oh."

"Really."

"That's interesting."

"This seems important to you."

Phrases that solicit more information

"Tell me more."

"Let's talk about it."

"Tell me the whole story."

KEEPING THE DOOR OPEN

Once you have opened the door, and the conversation has started, the goal is to keep the door open. This can be difficult, when you or the other person stumbles over something that is frightening. Here are some tools that can help you keep the conversation going, when the other person is afraid to go on, or has come to a dead end.

Open-ended questions

Open-ended questions are questions that cannot be answered with "Yes" or "No" or some other monosyllable. They usually begin with one of the following words:

How… (How did you do that?)

Who… (Who was at the party?)

What… (What is the matter with that?)

When… (When did that happen?)

Where… (Where was that?)

Tell me more.

What about "Why…?"

The word "why" is loaded. "Why did you do that?" can have a totally different meaning, depending on how it is said. Depending on your tone of voice, it can mean, "How could you be so stupid?" or it can mean, "What was your reason?" Remember that one of the four elements of acceptance is to be curious. So if you use "Why…" to start a question, be sure it's because you're curious about my motivation, not because you are judging me. Your tone of voice will communicate your intention.

Dealing with blame, accusation or disbelief

When someone is blaming you or accusing you unfairly, your first reaction will be to deny things. But starting a frustrating circle of "Yes you did" and "No I didn't" isn't very effective. Instead, it's usually helpful to take a deep breath and ask him, "How do you know that?" or, "What makes you think that?" These same questions can be helpful when he is making a statement that you don't believe is true. The goal of these questions is to move the focus of the conversation away from individual uncertainties into the possibility of looking together at facts and evidence that can be shared.

How do you feel about that?

Sometimes it's much easier for the other person to talk about facts and focus on information than to explore her feelings. But her hidden feelings may be causing some conflicts or preventing her from making wise choices. One way to help her explore her feelings is simply to ask her how she feels about this issue. Or you can ask simply, "How is that for you?"

Paraphrase

When he is telling a long story, it's sometimes useful to paraphrase what he's said in a few sentences, using your response to focus the story and keep it relevant. Paraphrasing can help to keep both of you interested.

Reflecting

Reflecting is a powerful way to support someone who is exploring. It may be the most important tool we have because as human beings, we have few opportunities to see our minds or hearts reflected in a mirror. We often depend on other people to mirror our feelings or thoughts. When people who love us interpret what is in our minds, we can see ourselves more clearly.

If you and I were in an active listening session, I could begin to reflect you by repeating exactly the word or phrase that you used. This may feel awkward at first, but for you it can be useful. It helps you listen to yourself. It builds a transparent bridge between your messages that can help you keep track of what you were trying to say. And it reassures you that I am listening—and accepting you.

Gradually, I could expand this reflecting to include, not what you have said exactly, but what I have heard you say. That is, I could tell you what I believe you really intended, or wished, to say. Or what was too painful to say. For instance, if you say, "I thought you were going to hit me," I might reflect by saying, "You thought I couldn't control myself."

On a deeper level, I can listen for qualities of grief or sorrow or other hidden emotions. I may sense a feeling that is hard to express in words, or that you may not be aware of, and I can respond by simply naming the feeling, and accepting it. Emotions are part of what makes us human, and to share them with another person is one of life's greatest comforts.

Check the accuracy of your understanding

Most arguments start with a misunderstanding. To make sure you understand what the other person is saying, pay attention to your own mind while you listen. As soon as you start to feel confused, you can stop and say, "I'm confused," and ask her to clarify whatever it is. Or you can say, "This is what I hear you saying. Is that right?"

Sometimes, when communication is very tense, you can prevent misunderstandings by reversing this process: you can ask the other person, "What did I just say?" It can be surprising to hear how your words were interpreted—or totally ignored.

SUMMARY OF ACTIVE LISTENING

Active listening is the primary tool that people in respectful relationships use to solve problems. Because we are using many facets of ourselves while listening—mind, heart, body and spirit—active listening can be called the Phillips screwdriver in our toolbox. We will use it especially when one of us feels troubled, and we need to feel that we can impact our environment. When something in the playground has gone wrong—we were attuned but our attunement has been disrupted—active listening is often how we begin to re-attune. This tool is also an excellent way to keep intimate relationships in good shape. If it's used often for the minor disruptions, it can prevent major disruptions.

To practice active listening, you pay attention to what the other person is saying—or trying to say. The primary listening tool is to pay attention to his body language. Additional tools can help you communicate that you are listening, you want him to speak, and you understand what he is saying.

Active listening can be used with anyone to get to know her better. And any time you are confronted with an unexpected hostility or insult, you can use the methods of active listening to prevent further misunderstanding or resolve the problem.

Summary of maintaining a respectful relationship

The playground is like a landscape in the mind. We travel across this landscape by building roads of respectful communication, and we need to maintain these roads to keep the relationship alive.

When we are attuned with each other, this road is like a freeway. Listening and responding, practicing respect and reciprocity, we seem to be singing the same tune.

But then the inevitable happens: the relationship is disrupted, and we feel that we're no longer singing the same tune, or one of us is off key. This disruption becomes an opportunity to re-evaluate the relationship and choose to re-commit.

If we decide to re-commit, we will need to re-attune. If we are confronting an issue that is difficult to talk about, we will need to practice active listening, adopt an attitude of acceptance, and make the effort to learn more—both about the other person, and about ourselves.

Active listening is a wonderful tool. We don't need to wait for a problem to emerge. We can use this tool to make our relationship more alive, because active listening can help us carry on a slow, intense and very satisfying conversation. During such a conversation, a respectful relationship can grow—and it can bloom.

Questions about maintaining the respectful relationship

What listening tool is like a flat head screwdriver?

Why does the road get bumpy when we're traveling across the landscape of the playground?

What are the three parts of the attachment sequence?

What phases in the attachment sequence make the glue that strengthens attachment? Why do these phases make attachments stronger?

Why is active listening like a Phillips screwdriver?

What are the four elements of the accepting attitude?

Name some door openers.

Name some ways to keep the door open.

Why is active listening hard to learn?

Why is active listening like love?

PART III

HABITS THAT DAMAGE RELATIONSHIPS

OUR HABITS

PEOPLE INVOLVED IN insecure (intrusive/dismissive, preoccupied/neglectful or disorganized) relationships have problems staying together. Their relationships are like tents—temporary encampments that break apart during the first storm.

However people involved in respectful relationships, who follow the rules of the playground and keep their relationship alive with smooth roads of communication, will probably stay together as long as they want to. Like a house built with good materials on a secure foundation, the respectful relationship withstands most pressures, both internal and external.

Although the playground provides a secure way for people to relate to each other, the people involved may sometimes feel insecure. This happens because ninety-nine percent of the time, human beings are acting out of habit. We depend upon our habits to get us through the day. Our behavior is habitual, and so are the ways we think, the ways we see the world, and the ways we relate to others. And all of us bring into any relationship all of our bad habits, as well as our good ones.

What is the difference between a good habit and a bad habit? From day to day our good habits help us to get where we want to go. Bad habits will trip us, and keep us trapped, stuck in a rut. Bad habits are like debris and cockroaches that we stumble over in the dark. By the time we recognize them, they've already done their damage. They may disgust us or frighten us. They can ruin our lives, or they can provide us with the opportunity to grow and change. One of our never-ending jobs in life is to become aware of our bad habits, and convert them into good habits.

A bad habit will often appear when an internal conflict—that split second when we're experiencing two (or more) opposing desires—causes a bad feeling. Usually one desire is for a quick, short-term goal, and another desire is for a longer-term goal. For example, maybe I've just been betrayed, and I want to lash out and break the relationship; but I also value the relationship and want to keep communication open.

During these split seconds we have the opportunity to convert a bad habit into a good one. Whenever we experience internal conflict, we can give ourselves a chance to respond—to think before we act. We can consider alternatives and make a choice, instead of acting out of habit. Gradually, as we repeat this process, we will develop a new, better habit to replace the old one.

Some of us were engaged in insecure relationships in the past, and now we find ourselves falling into the habit of seeing the other person through the template of that former relationship style. These habits can become so ingrained that they're invisible, and very hard to break. They will erode a good relationship. Like a nest of termites, they can silently and invisibly eat away at the foundation of the playground, until the stability of the relationship is threatened.

BOUNDARIES

ONE OF THE most common habits that erode relationships is failing to draw firm boundaries. Many people are afraid of boundaries. They may believe that drawing a firm boundary is a form of rejection. Or it feels selfish. Or they're afraid a boundary will isolate them—like a tall fence.

What is a boundary? Physically, my boundary begins with my skin. It begins when I let you know, either with a gesture or with words, how close you can be—whether you may touch me, or how you may touch me.

The boundary of my mind is like a virtual skin. Freud described the skin of the mind as an orange rind, studded with receptors and filters that are like security officers. These receptors and filters protect the mind from noticing too much noise and light; they also monitor and organize what the mind lets in, or perceives. This is a rind of habitual perceiving that prevents anything unexpected from entering the mind, and keeps us from feeling overwhelmed.

Some people have thin skins and some have thicker skins. Sensitive people may quickly react to subtle changes in light or noise, or be distracted by chaos. They may take things personally and get easily hurt.

People with thick skins can walk down a busy street and not even notice the lights or noise; they may crave chaos and stimulation. They may not even be aware of someone's attempt to control or hurt them.

HOW I DRAW BOUNDARIES

Inside the mind, the "I" creates a third boundary. The "I" occupies a kind of corner office, from where it manages all the emotions and thoughts and beliefs that are constantly interacting with the environment or each other. To keep the mind functioning, the "I" constantly chooses which thought, feeling or belief to focus on, and then connects it to what's going on in the environment. As we mature, we strengthen the "I" boundary, creating a peaceful place for this manager to work.

My "I" has been with me since I was an infant, and has developed definite desires, preferences and limits. As I get involved in a relationship with you, my "I" chooses what kinds of behavior I will tolerate, and what kinds I will not allow.

But sometimes I don't like what my "I" is choosing. If I'm feeling physically attracted to you, I don't want to hear my "I" whisper, "Don't let this guy touch you yet." When there's an internal conflict like this, it takes a certain effort—and courage—for me to accept this choice. Accepting this choice is one way I strengthen the "I" boundary. Expressing the choice is how I draw boundaries.

To draw a firm boundary, first I need to know which games I want to play—and which ones I really don't like. Then I can express my wishes in ways that invite people to play with me respectfully. Drawing my boundary is not a way of rejecting you. It's a way of communicating who I am. If you're interested, I'll tell you what I want. If your behavior is offensive, I will let you know.

COURAGE AND SKILL

What kind of courage does it take to draw a firm boundary? It's the kind we usually have instinctively as children, when we enter our first real playground, and we know why we're there. We approach the swings with intensity and focus, ready to play with all our might. We're going to explore this equipment, and how it works. We know which games we want to play, and with whom we want to play. In this first playground we sometimes got involved in conflicts or failed. We probably encountered bullies—people who didn't respect our boundaries. If we didn't learn then, we can learn later how to keep our courage in adversity and avoid or protect ourselves from bullies.

Later, we will look at negotiating skills. If we use negotiating along with our listening skills, we can stay brave. While we're making our way through the rough and tumble competition and pressure of work, family and romance, negotiating and listening give us methods to control our emotions and listen to our "I." And it's only when we listen to our "I" that we can maintain our boundaries. Maintaining our boundaries is an extension of one of the rules of respectful relationships: "I can take care of myself."

What kind of courage does it take to draw a firm boundary? It's the kind we usually have instinctively as children, when we enter our first real playground, and we know why we're there.

TAKING CARE OF MYSELF

Taking care of myself by drawing my boundary does not mean that I'm selfish or greedy. It means that I take some time and devote energy to knowing and reaffirming who I am. It means that when I step into a relationship, I maintain my balance, so that I'm not blown down by the first gust of wind. Keeping my balance means that I'm going in the direction I choose, but I'm also recognizing the limits of reality and the limits of the other person. I find ways to get where I'm going within these limits. That is, I adapt to reality. This is no easy task. First, it's hard to see the reality. And reality can give me some tough challenges. I can get so involved in adapting to reality that I forget where I was going or what was important.

In short, I take care of myself by doing my best to stay in control of myself and to choose how to behave. And in the respectful relationship, I not only accept my limits, but I'm also willing to learn my limits. Every day, new experiences will give me a chance to learn how much I can—and cannot—tolerate. And I will build these lessons into my understanding of myself.

The dance of boundaries: setting limits

Meanwhile, I'm also learning to see, and to adapt to, the other person's limits. This dance—of seeing and adapting to our own and to each other's limits—is the most basic game in the respectful relationship. This is the dance of boundaries. Learning to communicate our limits with each other in respectful ways is the most basic tool we use—as basic as the hammer.

Many people know only one way to communicate a limit: they set an ultimatum. They say, "If you do (or don't do) this again, we're through." But setting an ultimatum is like using a sledgehammer to drive a simple nail. It doesn't work well, and it can quickly break an otherwise secure relationship.

Communicating a limit can actually be very simple. Just as we do with toddlers, we can very effectively communicate a limit with nonverbal language. I can shake my head, No. I can turn away. I can stop playing our game.

Using words can also be simple. There are many ways to say "No." For example:

WAYS TO SAY "NO"

"That doesn't work for me."   "I don't want to."

"That's not respectful."   "It's not okay."

If necessary, I can take a time out and just be alone for a while. I can think about the message I've been trying to communicate: have I been clear and consistent? If I still need to set a limit, I can tell the other person,

"When you're ready to respect me and respect my limits, I will return."

Reaching these moments when one person or the other has transgressed a limit can feel like a crisis. But in fact, it can be a rich opportunity. It can be just the right time to use active listening. While the experience is fresh, you can take some time to listen to each other—learn new things about yourself and the other person, and why you behave as you do.

PATIENCE

One of the most important things to remember, while you're learning the dance of boundaries with each other, is to be patient. Just like a weather forecast, the stated intention of the other person may not always be believable. You can't always trust she will do what she says she will do, or know what her words really mean. Like her intentions, the morning forecast may be for a sunny day, and all you see is fog and clouds. Sometimes the forecast may be wrong. But often, in the afternoon, the sun will appear.

When the other person is having trouble hearing or seeing one of your limits, it may be hard to remember that he really wants to be in this relationship, and he intends to find a way to adapt. In the meantime, the weather in the relationship is unstable. During this time you may find it useful to repeat yourself: express your limit several times. Perhaps you could find a more effective or direct way to communicate your limit. Or you may just need to be patient—and wait. You cannot make the sun appear before it is ready.

SLOW DOWN: SEEING MORE OBJECTIVELY

At the end of the day, when the sun doesn't come out, and you realize the weather forecast was wrong, you may begin to see that the problem in this relationship is bigger than you thought it was. At this time, the first thing to do is to slow down. Slow down, and get out of habit mode. This is the time to look more closely at your own participation in this relationship. How much of the problem might belong to you? How much is buried, complex or even unchangeable?

When you find that your usual, habitual ways of dealing with problems isn't working, it does not mean the relationship is broken. It does mean that you need to slow down. You need to find another way to see the problem. Your subjective, habitual way of seeing things may not be accurate. When the problem is big and unusual, you may need to find an objective way of seeing the problem.

Objectivity is not difficult, but it is unfamiliar. Here is a simple outline of how to see a problem with objectivity:

SEEING A PROBLEM WITH OBJECTIVITY

1) Describe the problem to yourself in a way that a stranger could see it.

2) This means, describe the problem in terms of behavior. You aren't describing the reasons for the behavior or the feelings or thoughts that might be a problem. You are only describing the behavior that a stranger could see.

3) Describe the behavior in a way that is measurable: the intensity, the frequency, and its pervasiveness. How loud or violent is the behavior? How much trouble does it cause? Does it happen all the time, or only sometimes? If it happens only sometimes, exactly when does it happen?

For example, my problem may be, "He's neglecting me." An objective description of his behavior, so a stranger could see it, would be much more detailed: After dinner, he sits down with the newspaper and falls asleep until I awaken him. Then he's wide-awake and watches television, while I'm falling asleep. This happens every evening except Saturday and Sunday.

With this kind of objectivity, new clues emerge that can help me redefine my problem. Since his neglect happens only during the workweek, what feels like neglect may be in fact simple fatigue. Maybe he's tired from the day's work, and needs a little nap before dinner? We can imagine what kind of conversations might help us solve the problem.

CONTENT VS. RELATIONSHIP

Sometimes a relationship can fracture because we become focused on the content of problems, and we forget what is really important. When someone has borrowed my favorite sweater and then lost it, my tendency might be to focus on the lost sweater. In my conversations with this person, I might try to blame her, or worry that she'll lose something else.

But in fact, the problem is usually not the sweater. Unlike a person, my sweater, even if it were irreplaceable, would never be able to learn from me or teach me. And it couldn't return my love. Negotiating effectively about a lost sweater could actually become an opportunity to turn a stagnating relationship into one that is more alive. It's the relationship that is important.

When you feel the relationship is becoming unstable or unfriendly, it's always a good time to look at yourself, and ask, Why am I in this relationship? What do I really want? Am I doing something that is damaging this relationship? Am I doing my best to stay balanced? Am I communicating my limits effectively? Am I listening?

Summary of boundaries

Although the playground provides a secure way for people to relate to each other, our bad habits can make us feel insecure. This happens because ninety-nine percent of the time, human beings are acting out of habit. Just as our behavior is habitual, so are the ways we think, and the ways we relate to others.

One of the most common bad habits is a failure to draw firm boundaries. Drawing a boundary does not mean rejecting or withdrawing love. It means that we are willing to learn—and to express—what we want and prefer. We know instinctively how to draw boundaries when we are young children, and it can take courage and skill to continue drawing them as we grow older.

In the playground, one of the most basic games we play together is the dance of boundaries: setting limits with each other. Setting a limit can be as simple as saying "No." But when another person's transgression feels like a crisis, setting a limit may include a long conversation, and may be a good opportunity for both people to use some active listening. The dance of boundaries can take a lot of patience.

In the end, if the problem seems big and complex, it's probably time to try to see things differently: to become more objective. When we're more objective, we see the problem as a set of behaviors that we describe so that even a stranger could see them. Describe the intensity, frequency and pervasiveness of these behaviors.

Seeing the problem objectively can often help us solve the problem. But because we are human beings, we can't always grasp our reasons for tolerating or not tolerating certain behaviors in any particular relationship. The most important question to ask is, "Do I want to be in this relationship?" If the answer is yes, then these difficult questions about limits are simply part of the dance of boundaries.

Questions about boundaries

What is a boundary?

How do we protect ourselves from bullies?

What is the dance of boundaries?

Name three statements that will set a limit.

When do we need to see a problem more objectively? How do we do that?

ANGER

WE SAW THAT failing to draw firm boundaries is one bad habit that erodes the foundation of the playground. Failing to manage your anger is another one. Many people habitually allow their anger to escalate until it is out of control—and then regret the consequence. Others allow their anger to simmer at a low level, sometimes for years. The consequence of unmanaged anger is that good relationships are damaged or destroyed. People sometimes feel their anger comes out of the blue and takes over. They blame the anger, not themselves, for losing one good friend or lover after another.

What is anger? Anger is an emotion, but it's not a primary emotion. Although we may not be aware of it, anger is rarely our first reaction to a problem. Rather, anger is usually a reaction to another emotion—an emotion that is so bad we don't want to feel it. We get angry when we don't want to feel that bad emotion.

The most common emotions that cause anger are Weakness, Sadness, Fear and Confusion. These feelings are bad because they strip us of our confidence. When they take over the body, we feel physically ineffective. We may feel a sinking sensation or feel lightheaded. Sometimes we lose control of our bladder or bowels. We will trip over ourselves, drop things, or become lethargic or jittery. We can get constipated or nauseous. Our head may ache, our pulse races. In short, we feel bad.

However, when we let this bad feeling trigger anger, a surge of power replaces all that bumbling and loss of confidence—sometimes within a microsecond. We get angry so we don't have to feel bad.

In the list that follows, bad feelings are organized into categories. Like a thermometer, they rise from the mildest form of each category at the bottom, to the most intense form at the top.

FEELINGS THAT CAUSE ANGER

WEAKNESS	SADNESS	FEAR	CONFUSION
Powerless	Grieved	Desperate	Baffled
Unfit	Anguished	Panicky	Bewildered
Helpless	Depressed	Terrified	Perplexed
Vulnerable	Dispirited	Apprehensive	Lost
Weak	Sad	Frightened	Confused
Ineffective	Disappointed	Scared	Curious
Awkward	Out of sorts	On edge	Vague
Uncoordinated	Low	Nervous	Unsure
		Worried	Undecided

Angry feelings also vary. Again, like a thermometer, they're listed with the mildest form at the bottom, and the most intense form at the top.

ANGER

Enraged

Seething

Furious

Fed up

Frustrated

Mad

Resentful

Annoyed

Irritated

THE INTENSITY FORMULA

Here is a formula about anger: the intensity of my anger will equal the intensity of the bad emotion I am trying to suppress. If I am feeling un-coordinated, I may get irritated. However, if I am feeling powerless, that utterly horrible sinking sensation throughout the whole body, I will react with a surge of rage. Because the bad feeling can transform into anger so quickly, it's often hard to identify which feeling is actually causing the anger. But you can find a clue to how intense the bad feeling is by measuring the intensity of your anger.

FROM WORDS TO ACTION

Milder emotions can be expressed in words. While I'm feeling irritated or annoyed, it's not that difficult to tell the other person, "When you do that, I get annoyed."

However, more intense emotions are much harder to express in words. To express these intense emotions, we are likely to act out. When we feel seething or enraged, we will throw a tantrum, become manipulative, with-draw and avoid the other person, become self-destructive, or strike out physically.

EXPRESSING ANGER

Anger is a physical phenomenon. It holds onto the body. Even when I'm irritated or annoyed, I feel tense and my temperature has gotten hot-ter and my fists clench. Often, I need to express this annoyance physically before I can think straight. And as anger becomes more intense, the need to express it physically becomes more immediate and the expression needs to be more intense.

How can we express anger without hurting ourselves or someone else, and without damaging the relationship? Keep in mind that your anger be-longs to you, and expressing it doesn't mean dumping it onto someone else. Expressing anger is something we need to do by ourselves.

When I'm annoyed, I'll get up and sharpen some pencils, or go for a walk or run, pace, wash the dishes. There are as many different ways of expressing anger as there are moments and people experiencing the anger. Some people beat their pillows. They scream, yell or moan. Kick. Stomp. Cry. Weed the garden. Pull hair. Dig a hole. Split firewood.

The list is long, but it is not endless. It stops at expressions that hurt yourself or someone else. And the intensity of the expression needs to match the intensity of the anger. Washing dishes won't help when you are feeling enraged. If you need to yell, go outside or find a pillow to yell into—don't yell at someone else. When you're searching for a way to express your anger, it helps to find or make some time alone. Once you find a good way, make that expression a habit so you don't have to think about it, because it's often impossible to think when you're angry.

RESENTMENT

Anger transforms bad feelings into a surge of power that is, like fire, raw energy—a physical energy that we can use. If we don't get rid of the energy by expressing it, we need to use it. Either we use it in a positive way—harness it to focus and act constructively—or the anger will use us.

Some people don't get rid of their anger but instead hold onto it: they feel a low level resentment. For instance, a man may feel trapped in a relationship with a woman who isn't respectful—maybe he feels devalued or misused. He knows that she doesn't care enough to change her behavior so, rather than try to talk with her, he maintains a constant feeling of resentment toward her.

This resentment becomes like a warm fire inside of him, and every snide comment she makes becomes another log he puts on that fire. Over time, he doesn't want to let the fire go out. It becomes a valuable warm place, a state he can dwell in and energy he can draw from, whenever he feels lonely or weary.

People often rely on resentment to keep them attached in insecure relationships. It can keep people attached to an irritating person long after that person has left or died. Feeding that low-level fire with bad feelings can become an entrenched, life-long habit that prevents people from avoiding whatever is causing the resentment in the first place.

RECOGNIZING THE BAD FEELING

How can you avoid the bad feelings that cause anger? Ideally, you would use your anger as a signal that something was awry in the relationship. As soon as you began to feel angry, you would take time to recognize the feeling causing the anger. Just that act—naming the bad feeling—would reduce its intensity.

After you recognized the bad feeling, you would let yourself feel bad for a while: tolerate the bad feeling instead of letting it cause anger. You would let the bad feeling motivate you to think about the circumstances causing this dilemma, work at seeing the problem differently, and eventually arrive at a way to resolve the problem.

The anger thermometer

Although the ideal way to manage anger is to avoid it entirely—recognize the bad feeling instead—this would require us to think, and often anger happens so quickly we don't have a chance to think. So we need a way to manage anger—keep it from causing harm.

As soon as we start to feel angry, we know we're headed for trouble. But the feeling of anger itself isn't what causes problems. What causes problems is not controlling that anger, and letting it drive us into destructive behavior. When we're angry we will make mistakes. Get into trouble.

The more intense our anger is, the more difficult it will be to control it, and the more serious the trouble will be. People who can't control their anger often wish they could. They can spend a lifetime paying for their behavior in one angry minute. When someone is ready to stop letting anger get them into trouble, they are ready to use the Anger Thermometer.

You will find the Anger Thermometer on the next two pages. Making a copy of it—to look at while your read the instructions—might make it easier to understand.

THE ANGER THERMOMETER

	WHAT MAKES ME FEEL THIS WAY?	HOW DO I BEHAVE?
Boiling		
Really Angry		
Upset		
Annoyed		
Calm		

PHYSICAL SIGNS	THOUGHTS	HOW COULD I GAIN CONTROL?

Many people believe that, once they begin to feel angry, their anger is in control. They believe anger has to escalate until they explode. Often, they weren't even aware something was wrong while they were feeling the milder forms of anger—irritation or annoyance. By the time they became aware of their anger, they were already upset, and it was very difficult to calm down. As a result, they grew up believing that anger has to escalate, once it begins.

But in fact, the best way to control anger is to become aware of it while it is still a mild emotion. While anger is mild, it is much easier to control, and if you control it at this point you can prevent the trouble that happens when you let anger escalate.

FINDING CALM

The Thermometer is divided into five different questions, outlined at the top of the page. To use it, begin with the question at the top of the column, "What makes me feel this?"

Look at the bottom of the page. Ask yourself, What makes me feel calm? This is not an easy question, because calm means different things to different people. Here are some different meanings of calm: I can think straight. I'm relaxed. I'm at peace. I'm focused.

Think about what calm means to you, and then think about the question, What makes me feel calm? Write your answers in the column, next to the word CALM. Some people feel calm when they listen to music, go for a walk, talk with a friend, etc.

Now, ask yourself the question in the next column: "How do I behave?" How do I behave when I'm calm? Write your answers in the square. Do you smile more? Are you more sociable? Are you more likely to cook or play a musical instrument?

Now move to the square in the next column, "Physical Signs." What are the physical signs that you are calm? What happens to your muscles? Your heart rate? Breathing? Write your answers in the square of that column.

The next question, to the right of "Physical Signs" is about "Thoughts." What kind of thoughts do you have when you are calm? What do you think about yourself, your family, your friends, your future?

CALM IS POWER

Spend a lot of time on the CALM section. Understand calmness as well as you can. Recognize when you are calm, and what makes you feel calm.

Calmness is your primary weapon in your war with anger. With calmness on your side, you will stop letting anger steal your energy, and you will begin arming yourself with your own power.

It is only when I am calm that I am powerful. When I am calm, I am effective. I can think straight. I can see the problem, and be creative about how to remove or bypass obstacles. When I am calm I can believe that no matter what challenges life hands me, I will be able to figure out a way to take care of myself.

NEXT, LOOK AT ANNOYED

After you are very sure of what makes you feel calm, and that feeling calm is a very good thing, you are ready to move up the thermometer. Think of yourself as being in a library or at a desk absorbed in what you are reading, and the person next to you begins to tap his fingers on the table. Most people would find this annoying.

Ask yourself, "What makes me feel annoyed?" Most people are annoyed when they are interrupted. Write your answers in the column next to ANNOYED. Some people get annoyed when they are too hot or too cold. Look at the feeling chart and ask yourself, How angry do I get when I'm feeling disappointed? Worried? Ask yourself, How angry do I get when I can't control the other person's behavior? Write down the feelings and situations that bring you out of that delicious feeling of calm, and get you annoyed.

Now, move to the next column: How do you behave when you are annoyed? Write your answers in the box. Are you more likely to be rude? Short with people? Withdrawn?

Move to the next column and write down the "Physical Signs." How do you know you are annoyed? Does your head start to spin? Do you clench your fists? Does your temperature rise? Your breathing grow shallow?

Next, write down some of the thoughts you have when you're annoyed. "That person has to stop" is a common thought. Some people, at this point, are afraid they might lose their temper. You might feel guilty.

GET BACK TO CALM

Now comes the most important question in this whole process: "How could I gain control?" How can I get back down to CALM? You might think the solution is to express your annoyance physically, but a physical expression is not the solution. Expressing anger physically only begins the process of relieving anger's hold on your body so that you can open your mind and think about the problem. To finally get back down to CALM, you will need to look at and possibly solve the problem that is causing the annoyance.

Here are some ways to get back down to CALM: you might ask the person to stop. You might use an "I" statement. You might re-focus—think about something interesting or fun. Ignore the person. Avoid situations that are annoying. You might listen to some music or go for a walk.

Write down all the options you can think of, and ask other people for some help.

LOOK AT UPSET

Notice: it is much easier to get back to calm now, than it would be later. If you let yourself continue to feel annoyed, the very next thing that happens—no matter how small—can push you up the thermometer into UPSET.

Go through the same process, now, with the questions about being upset. What makes you feel upset? How do you behave when you're upset? What are the physical signs that you're upset? What kinds of thoughts do you have when you're upset? And how can you gain control?

When you are upset, it's harder to gain control, and get back to calm. You may need some help from a friend or family member. You may need to leave the scene, take a time-out.

SUMMARY OF ANGER THERMOMETER

Realistically, we cannot avoid anger in our lives. But as you continue working on the Thermometer, you will notice that anger does not need to escalate. It doesn't need to get so intense that it becomes destructive. In fact, the opposite is true: feeling annoyed is a gift from the body—a physical sign that something is wrong. It's a signal that says, "Get calm as soon as possible."

The way to stay out of trouble is to stay calm. It is when we are calm that we can think. We can think about what we want in the long term, and make plans for how to get it. We are more likely to enjoy our friends and ourselves. While we are calm, we can use words to communicate and express ourselves, and we are more likely to maintain and enjoy our respectful relationships. The best way to stay calm is do things that make us feel calm, and avoid situations that make us irritated or upset. But this is much easier said than done. If we can't avoid situations that make us upset, we can at least learn to think before we act. Instead of letting anger escalate, we can focus on finding the most effective way to get calm again.

Negotiating

How can you preserve the rules of the playground and stay respectful when you really disagree with the other person, or they have done something that makes you angry?

First of all, while you're feeling angry, you need to express the anger—physically. Alone. Get rid of that physical hold. You know you are getting close to the end of anger's physical hold when, while you are kicking or crying, you begin to think. You may want to get rid of this anger by dumping it onto the other person. Or you may want to complain.

What is the difference between dumping and complaining? Dumping is a form of blaming: I've been storing all my resentments and hurts in a mental backpack instead of dealing with them while they were only annoyances, and now this particular insult just escalated the annoyance to upset, and I want to blame someone. Unfortunately the person I'm dumping on doesn't want my anger.

Complaining, on the other hand, is one of the human being's most basic needs. The Lamentation is a song and poetry form dating from the beginning of history. We need to complain, if only to discover what is bothering us. One of life's greatest gifts is a friend who can listen to our complaints, and not react to them or try to give us advice, but instead affirm or reflect what we're thinking and feeling.

A RULE HAS BEEN BROKEN

When you're angry with someone in the playground, it could be because you disagree or are hurt. But underneath these problems, a rule has been broken. So when you are feeling angry ask yourself, which of my rules was broken?

Each of us brings our own rules into the relationship. As we've noted before, I need to know what my rules are—and what yours are—because inevitably, our rules will clash. When they clash, we will disagree.

Fortunately, most rules are not written in stone. Instead of blaming the other person, it's usually much more helpful to negotiate our rules. You can begin negotiating by asking the other person, "Why are you behaving that way?" Find out more about what she believes—and also what you believe. What are the beliefs underlying your rules?

Beliefs are important because we create our rules within our belief systems. Our beliefs organize our behavior. Once we both know what each other believes, we may be able to negotiate a shared belief system that can support behavior we both like.

"I" statements

When we're feeling angry, we often use the word "You." We want to blame the other person, saying "You did x…" or "You always…" or "You need to …." These are "You" statements. The problem with using "You" statements is that the other person doesn't hear them.

As soon as I hear the word "You" at the beginning of a sentence, my body tenses up. "You" means that someone is not talking to me, he is talking about me. When his tone of voice is angry or hostile, and his words presume that he knows what is going on inside my own private space, I cannot hear what he is saying. Instead, my mind is occupied with putting up boundaries, escaping or defending myself.

When a person begins a sentence with "You," he is not speaking about himself, and he has no authority. In fact, he is trying to take authority away from me. But when a sentence begins with "I...," the person speaking has full authority. When I say, "I want...," I am speaking with the full knowledge and experience of being myself and I am talking only about myself. No one can disagree with what I am saying.

The "I" statement is a technique that helps people negotiate disagreements and express intense emotions. "I" statements are simple to understand, but hard to use. They are statements beginning with the word "I." For example:
> "I believe..."
> "I want..."
> "I wish..." etc.

The big advantage to using "I" statements is that the other person is much more likely to hear what you're saying. When you talk about yourself, your feelings, your beliefs, your motivations, the other person is not busy putting up boundaries. She can keep her ears open. Also, because you are talking about yourself, "I" statements help her to understand you, and help you to understand yourself.

COMPLEX "I" STATEMENTS
A slightly more complex version of the "I" statement looks like this:
> "When you do (or say) X, I feel Y." For instance,
>> "When you talk about her like that, I feel jealous."
>> "When you behave like that, I get annoyed."

The more complex version of "I" statements can be useful when the problem has been going on for a while, and you've noticed a pattern. Identifying the pattern with this kind of "I" statement can be a very effective way of beginning to solve the problem.

SUMMARY OF "I" STATEMENTS

"I" statements begin with "I." They are hard to use, because they require us to think. Before I can open my mouth to use an "I" statement, I have to think about my feelings or beliefs, and find words to describe them. This is a sobering exercise, and one that can help me to take responsibility for my own participation in a problem.

"I" statements help us to take care of ourselves by forcing us to identify our own rules. When we've identified a pattern of behavior, we can use the more complex "I" statement. When we're angry or feeling intense emotions, "I" statements help us stay respectful in the playground.

ACTIVE LISTENING AND THE "I" STATEMENT

When a problem continues to emerge in a relationship, you can combine active listening with the "I" statement to make both tools more effective. When someone isn't responding to your "I" statement, or the "I" statement alone isn't solving the problem, it's time to ask the person to discuss things. Apparently the problem is more complex or deeper than you thought it was. You can prepare for the active listening session by looking at the problem objectively. Then, during the session, present your understanding of the problem, and ask the other person for his, and listen carefully. Use listening and "I" statements to try to see the problem from another perspective.

Frustration

Frustration could be seen as a form of anger, but it can also be seen as a slightly different emotion. While anger is a reaction to a bad feeling, frustration is a reaction to being thwarted. We get frustrated when we are trying to accomplish something and we cannot succeed. We're faced with a brick wall and we run into it—and keep running into it. The more we hit the wall, the more frustrated we get, and frustration can escalate to the boiling point.

Another way of describing frustration is to say that it happens when we don't ask the right question. Imagine yourself trying to tighten a flat head screw—but you're using a Phillips screwdriver, and the question you're asking is, "What's wrong with this screw?"

While you're in the grip of frustration, you can't think straight. But recognizing and naming a feeling can immediately reduce its grip, so develop this habit: as soon as you've tried the same method three times without success say, "I'm feeling frustrated!"

HOW TO RESOLVE FRUSTRATION

1) Once you can think straight, look at the problem. What is making me so frustrated? Try to understand and name the problem as well as you can. For instance,
   "She's not listening to me."
   "The engine won't start."
2) Look at what you are doing. What tool are you using? Maybe you're yelling at her, or continuing to turn the ignition.
3) Ask yourself, "What do I want?" What is your goal? Do you want her to listen? What do you want to accomplish? Do you want to start the engine? What do you want the outcome to be?
4) Ask yourself, "What am I doing wrong? Why isn't my method working?" Well, you might consider, she isn't listening because I'm yelling. Maybe the battery is dead.
5) Ask, "What would work better?" Maybe, if I spoke in a calm voice and used respectful language, she would be more likely to listen. Maybe I could test the battery.

Shame

Among the bad feelings, shame is probably the worst one, and the most intense kind of anger is the reaction to shame. Shame is a feeling so destructive it can kill. Most people who experience shame can't even feel it for more than a split second because it hurts too much.

When we've made a mistake and we're suddenly faced with the consequence, there are two different ways to react: we can feel guilt, or we can feel shame.

It is easy to confuse shame with guilt. But in fact, these two feelings are radically different. Guilt performs an important function in our society and in our lives. It is what we feel when we have broken one of our own rules. It is a bad feeling that helps us know when we've damaged a valuable relationship. It causes us to feel regret or remorse. When we feel guilty because we've damaged a relationship, we can repair the relationship by apologizing. After the relationship is repaired, and we're sure we won't make that mistake again, our guilt is gone.

Shame, on the other hand, performs no good function at all. Shame happens when we believe—or are told by someone we love—"You are worthless." Children feel shame when they are told by their parents, "I wish you'd never been born." Shame destroys a person's ability to participate in relationships or to receive love.

Why does shame happen? People make shaming statements about others when they, themselves, are feeling ashamed. In families, generation after generation, parents who feel ashamed of themselves use shaming statements to punish children for mistakes: "You idiot." "You can't do anything right." "You'll go to prison just like your grandpa."

Making a shaming statement will damage a respectful relationship immediately. If it continues, it will destroy the relationship. A person who feels shame is drowning. He cannot respect himself or others; he cannot reciprocate; he cannot participate in the playground.

On the following page is a picture of how guilt differs from shame:

THE DIFFERENCE BETWEEN GUILT & SHAME

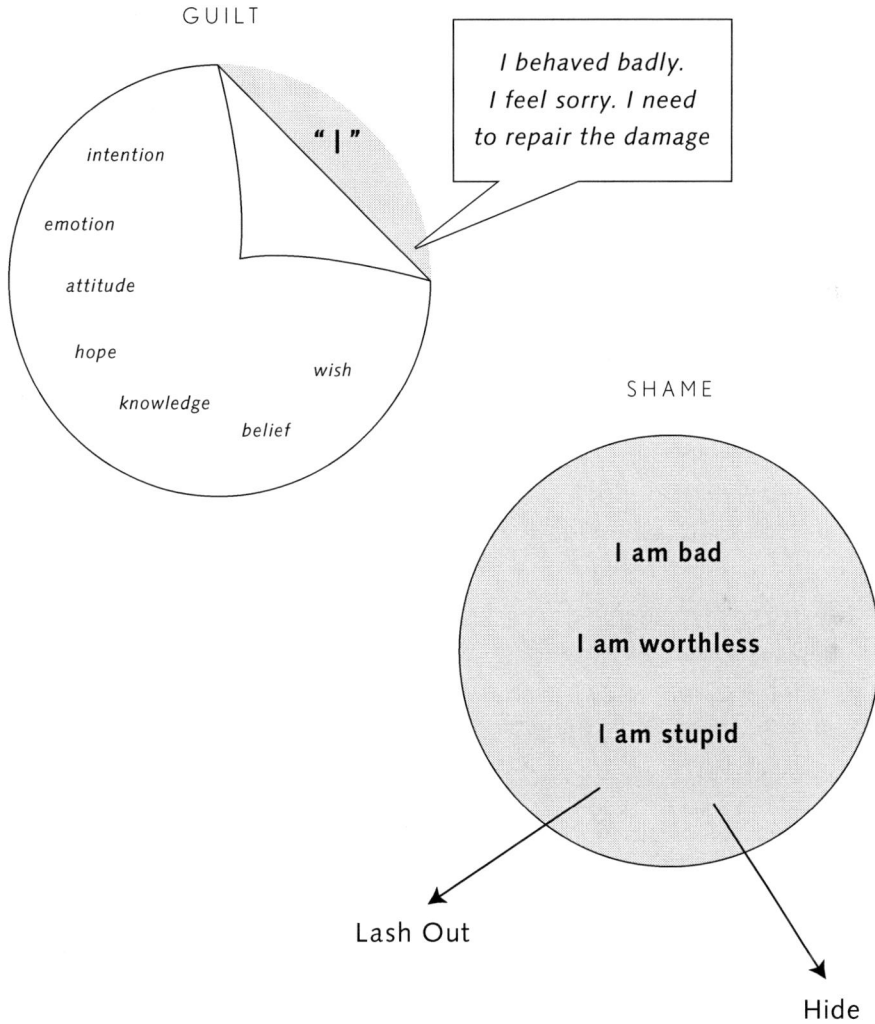

GUILT

intention

emotion

attitude

hope

knowledge   *wish*

belief

"I"

I behaved badly.
I feel sorry. I need
to repair the damage

SHAME

I am bad

I am worthless

I am stupid

Lash Out

Hide

BEHAVIOR VS. SELF

The biggest difference between guilt and shame is that when I'm feeling guilty, I am focused on the result of my behavior. But when I'm feeling shame, I'm focused on the lack of worth and lovability of my whole self.

When I'm feeling guilty and am focused on my bad behavior, I can see that I made a mistake. The guilt is not overwhelming. It does feel bad and it may be intense, but it doesn't totally destroy my sense of self. While I'm feeling guilty, my "I" can still observe and manage my emotions, thoughts, beliefs and motivations. I can still be aware of my intentions, control my attitude, and maintain my hope.

When I'm guilty, my "I" isn't overwhelmed because it knows that I can fix things. It's not the end of the world. I can apologize. I can make a promise and a plan to ensure that I don't make that mistake again.

But when I am feeling shame, I believe that the person I love hates me, or believes I'm a bad person. I feel utterly worthless. My "I" cannot operate—it's overwhelmed. My whole mind is flooded. Children who grow up in a state of shame don't develop an "I." They can't name their emotions, don't know their thoughts.

When a person is drowning in shame, there is no way for him to make an apology and repair the damage. His only choice is to escape the feeling, and the only ways to escape are to hide or lash out. If he tries to hide, he may isolate himself or hide behind lies, avoid eye contact, or leave. If he lashes out in reaction to shame he will feel the most intense anger there is. He can lash out against others, or he can lash out against himself. It is this kind of anger that causes people to kill themselves or others.

Because shame stunts and overwhelms the "I," people who want to stop drowning in this emotion usually benefit from getting some professional help. With psychotherapy, they can build an "I" that is strong enough to recognize shame when it appears, and choose whether to let this feeling overwhelm them. When they make a mistake, they may choose to feel guilty instead of feeling ashamed. They can acquire tools to help them repair damage and improve relationships. Changing a lifelong habit of reacting to mistakes by feeling overwhelmed with shame can be a long difficult process, but with some help it can be done.

Kinds of disruption

When a relationship is disrupted, the people separate. As we've seen before, disruption can be a healthy part of the attachment sequence: it can trigger re-attunement and strengthen the attachment. But certain kinds of disruptions can destroy even the most secure relationship.

When a disruption is caused by shame, there can be no re-attunement. The relationship is broken. When the disruption is caused by violence or brutality, it may be impossible for the people to ever re-attune.

When the disruption is too long—when a person disappears, and fails to keep in touch—the reunification can be very tense. Long distance relationships, when people have to stay attached without seeing each other, can be difficult to maintain. If both people work hard to stay in touch and are deeply committed, the re-attunement can be delicious. But when one or the other person has changed too much over time, sometimes it can be impossible to re-attune.

When the disruption is intense and happens too often, the foundation of the relationship may disintegrate. Addictions that steal a person away from the playground can destroy an otherwise respectful relationship. When one person repeatedly threatens to kill herself or abandon the relationship, even the most secure relationship will break.

Summary of anger

The habit of losing control of your anger can erode and even destroy a valuable relationship. Anger is almost always a reaction to a bad feeling, replacing that bad feeling with a surge of power. Anger itself can physically take hold of your body, so when you need to express your anger, it's often best to find something physical to do.

When you are ready to stop letting anger get you into trouble, you are ready to use the Anger Thermometer, a way of getting acquainted with both your anger and also the calmness that is your primary weapon against anger.

When you are in the playground with someone who is making you angry, it helps to take inventory of your beliefs and also her beliefs, because beliefs organize the rules that determine behavior. If you want to negotiate a shared belief system that can support more agreeable behavior, you can use "I" statements: statements that begin with the word "I." When you perceive a pattern of behavior that is causing trouble, you can use the more complex "I" statement.

Getting frustrated is another habit that causes trouble in relationships. We get frustrated when our method of solving a problem is not working. To resolve frustration we can look at both the problem and the method more closely and take time to think of an alternative method that might work better.

Reacting to our mistakes by falling into shame rather than feeling guilt is another habit that erodes and destroys relationships. Shame overwhelms the whole self so that we can't think and can't repair the relationship. But guilt helps us to change our behavior and repair the relationship.

Making a shaming statement can disrupt a respectful relationship in a way that is irreparable, and falling into shame can keep us out of the playground. When people disappear for too long, or their absences are too frequent, the relationship can be severely strained or broken.

Questions about anger

Name four emotions that cause anger.

What is the function of anger?

Is it a good idea to share anger?

Why is calmness our best weapon against anger?

What is the first question to ask when someone in the playground is making us angry?

List some "I" statements.

What are the five steps for resolving frustration?

What is the biggest difference between guilt and shame?

How does shame destroy a relationship?

STRESS

MOST DOCTORS AGREE that stress is at the root of disease, and I would add that stress is at the root of almost everything that goes wrong in relationships. But most people don't know what stress is. They believe that stress comes from doing too much. Although packing your schedule too tightly increases your pressure, the underlying source of stress is how you feel about what you're doing—and about yourself.

Jesus knew about stress many centuries ago. According to the apostle Thomas, when the disciples asked Jesus how to live, his answer was simple and direct: "Do not do what you hate."[7]

Doing what you hate is an accurate definition of the most destructive kind of stress. If you pay attention to your physical state—your muscles, heart rate, breathing, etc.—you will notice that when you spend time doing something you hate, you become tense and frustrated. Working at a job you hate or dealing for long periods with people you hate is an enormous strain on your body and your mind. And it can drain your capacity to pay attention. You can't respect yourself or others when you are doing what you hate.

Pressure can increase when we're working against a deadline, managing financial limits, dealing with a big loss or serious illness, or reeling from the ramifications of an accident. These are just a few of the many dilemmas that can make our usual tasks and roles feel overwhelming.

During stressful times, you may feel that all the different jobs and roles calling for your attention are like naughty children tugging at your shirt-sleeves. You may fall into a habit of becoming preoccupied and neglecting those children. Or you may feel these pressures are intrusive, invading your privacy; you may want to demand that they change or dismiss them.

You can fool your mind, but you can't fool your body. You first begin to feel destructive stress in the body, before it affects the mind.

Under stress, it's easy to regress into bad habits, and behave as though you and your work were in an insecure relationship. This insecure relationship will drain your energy. Your thoughts and memories may become increasingly intrusive or you can become un-controllably preoccupied during stressful times. If you hate the work or don't like the people, the stress can become destructive and make you ill.

The psychiatrist D. W. Winnicott has written that a mother does not have to be perfect; she only needs to be good enough.[8] During times of stress, this observation can be very comforting. As responsible adults, while our roles and jobs may feel like children demanding our attention, we don't have to pay full attention to all of them all the time. We just need to do a job that is good enough.

It can help to see your roles or jobs as individuals you need to respect, each one demanding a certain amount of time and energy. If you were in the playground with these individuals, you would respect each job or role (including the job of taking care of your body) for who she really was. You would negotiate with her to fit into a time schedule that left you feeling competent enough.

Thoughts, memories and feelings can also feel like demanding children, interrupting you or hanging around when you want to focus on some-thing. If you find your "I" is having trouble focusing, or you are becoming preoccupied, you might seek some professional help to strengthen the boundary of your "I."

When you see your thoughts, your work and your roles as individuals, and respect them for who they really are, you can change your behavior enough to manage the stress. If you love doing the work or find the other people stimulating, that stress can be invigorating.

DISCOVERING THE SOURCES OF STRESS

It's not easy to know what we hate, because we human beings are remarkably good at fooling ourselves. If we feel we have no choice, even when we hate what we're doing, we will find a way to believe we like it. Many people believe that they like their jobs, even when they come home feeling irritable and tense every day.

You can fool your mind, but you can't fool your body. You first begin to feel destructive stress in the body, before it affects the mind. So the most accurate way of discovering the origins of stress in your life is to pay attention to your body. Using the skills you learned while working on the Anger Thermometer, you can notice your physical reactions to certain people, situations and tasks. Become aware of how you behave when you're approaching stressful places. Do your thoughts change from being hopeful to becoming fearful or negative?

BALANCE REDUCES STRESS

In today's world, it's impossible to avoid stress. But most of the time, we can reduce stress to a manageable level by focusing on the opposite of stress, which is balance. We can bring balance to all facets of life.

For example, when you have to spend time doing what you hate, find a way to balance this situation by doing something uplifting and refreshing. When you find yourself dealing with a person you don't like, try to balance your judgments with generosity: find something about that person that is commendable or interesting. Use the skills you have learned in this book to invite people into respectful relationships. Bring respect and balance into all aspects of your life.

Summary of stress

Stress is at the root of almost everything that goes wrong in relationships, but the source of stress is less from doing too much than from feeling bad about what you are doing, or about yourself. Doing what you hate causes the most destructive form of stress. Stress can be reduced when you treat your work and responsibilities with respect—see how much time and energy each job really demands.

Too much stress can make us feel incompetent, but if we form the habit of relating to the different facets of our life in respectful ways, we will be much more likely to feel competent even under stress. Winnicott's observation can help us remember that we don't have to be perfect. We can negotiate with the jobs pressuring us—figure out how to fit them into a time schedule that leaves us feeling good enough.

We can fool our minds, but we can't fool our bodies. To discover the sources of stress, it helps to use the skills learned in the Anger Thermometer to monitor our body's reactions to various roles and responsibilities. Once we know the sources of our stress, we can balance those stresses with jobs or situations that are uplifting and refreshing. Most of all, it's important to relate to all people and all parts of our life with respect and reciprocity, and take good care of ourselves.

Questions about Stress

❖

What is the source of stress?

What is the most destructive kind of stress?

What was Winnicott's observation about being a mother?

What bad habit will make our jobs and roles more stressful?

How can we discover our sources of stress?

What is the opposite of stress?

CONCLUSION

Everyone benefits from respectful relationships

THE WORLD OF human relationships can be complex and challenging, but it can also be rich and exciting. Each human is unique, and so is each relationship. In this book, we have explored the qualities, habits and rules that can ensure that your relationships will be secure. In respectful relationships, you can nurture and be nurtured; you can anticipate support and find ways to solve problems. Using active listening, you can develop skills that serve you well in all the domains of your life. Setting limits, drawing boundaries, managing anger and reducing stress, you can prevent a great deal of grief.

Respectful relationships are simple to understand, but it takes commitment and effort to build them and keep them alive. Parents can bring their children into the playground. Not only you, but also your spouse, colleagues and friends can all benefit when you understand and commit yourself to a lifestyle of self-care, respect and reciprocity. When you follow the rules of the playground, you will build relationships that endure. You can respect yourself and feel happy with yourself and your life.

I'll end with a warning: respectful relationships can be contagious. As you build enduring relationships with people, you may find many people around you becoming more respectful. Your own perceptions may evolve: you may begin to see all human relationships as being part of a larger play-ground—where your partner is the planet that sustains you. You may wish to find more ways to respect the earth and to reciprocate—to give back to the environment it provides.

APPENDIX

References

ATTACHMENT

Bowlby, John (1969), *Attachment, Vol. 1 of Attachment and Loss*. and *Separation: Anxiety & Anger. Vol. 2 of Attachment and Loss*. London: Hogarth Press. New York: Basic Books; Harmondsworth: Penguin (1971)

Fonagy, Peter; Gergely, Gyorgy; Jurist, Elliot L.; Target, Mary (2002), *Affect Regulation, Mentalization, and the Development of the Self*. New York: Other Press

Hughes, Daniel (1998), *Building the Bonds of Attachment*. Northvale, NJ: Jason Aronson

Main, Mary (1993), "Discourse, Prediction, and Recent Studies in Attachment: Implications for Psychoanalysis," *Journal of the American Psychoanalytic Association* 41:209-244

Siegel, D. J. (1999), *The Developing Mind*. New York: Guilford

Stern, D. (1985), *The Interpersonal World of the Infant*. New York: Basic Books

Winnicott, D. W. (1964), *The Child, The Family, and the Outside World.* New York: Addison-Wesley

Winnicott, D. W. (1971), *Playing and Reality.* London: Routledge

PARENTING BOOKS

Archer, C. (1999), *First Steps in Parenting the Child Who Hurts.* London: Jessica Kingsley

Gray, D. (2002), *Attaching in Adoption.* Indianapolis, IN: Perspectives Press

Hughes, Daniel A. (2009), *Attachment-Focused Parenting: Effective Strategies to Care for Children.* New York: W. W. Norton & Co.

Keck, G. & Kupecky, R. M. (2002), *Parenting the Hurt Child.* Colorado Springs, CO: Pinon Press

FOR CHILDREN

Freymann, Saxton & Elffers, J. (1999), *How are you Peeling: Foods with Moods.* New York: Arthur A. Levine Books

ACTIVE LISTENING

Faber, Adele & Mazlish, Elaine (1999), *How to Talk So Kids Will Listen & Listen so Kids Will Talk.* New York: Avon Books

Gordon, Dr. Thomas (2000), *Parent Effectiveness Training: The tested new way to raise responsible children.* New York: Penguin Books

Nichols, Michael P. (2009), *The Lost Art of Listening: How Learning to Listen Can Improve Relationships.* New York, London: Guilford Press

Stone, Douglas & Patton, Bruce & Heen, Sheila (2000), *Difficult Conversations: How to Discuss What Matters Most*. New York: Viking

SHAME

Kaufman, Gersen (1980), *Shame: The Power of Caring*. Rochester, VT: Schenkman Books, Inc.

Nathanson, Donald L., *Shame and Pride*. London: W. W. Norton & Co., Ltd.

Endnotes

[1] D. W. Winnicott, *Playing and Reality*. (London: Routledge, 1971), 47-48.

[2] Mary Main, "Discourse, Prediction, and Recent Studies in Attachment: Implications for Psychoanalysis," *Journal of the American Psychoanalytic Association* 41:, 212.

[3] Main, M., & Hesse, E. (1990). Parents' unresolved traumatic experiences are related to infant disorganized attachment status: Is frightened/frightening parental behavior the linking mechanism? In M. T. Greenberg, D. Cicchetti, & E. M. Cummings (Eds.), *Attachment in the Preschool Years: Theory, Research, and Intervention*, 161-182. Chicago, IL: University of Chicago Press.

[4] Daniel A. Hughes, *Attachment—Focused Parenting: Effective Strategies to Care for Children*. (New York: W. W. Norton & Co., 2009), 11-12.

[5] Main, M., & Hesse, E.

[6] Daniel A. Hughes.

[7] *The Gospel According to Thomas*, trans. A. Guillaumont, H.-Ch. Puech, G. Quispel, W. Till and Y. 'Abd Al Masih. (New York: Harper & Row, 1959), 5.

[8] F. Robert Rodman, ed., *The Spontaneous Gesture: Selected Letters of D. W. Winnicott*. (London: H. Karnac (Books) Ltd., 1999), 38.

Mary McMillan lives in Lake County, California,
where she works as a Marriage and Family Therapist.
Her book of poetry, *This Wanting*, was published in 2008.